Painted Garden Furniture Projects

Areta Bingham

Sterling Publishing Co., Inc. New York
A Sterling / Chapelle Book

Chapelle, Ltd.:
- Owner: Jo Packham
- Editor: Leslie Farmer
- Photography: Kevin Dilley for Hazen Photography
  and Scot Zimmerman
- Staff: Kass Burchett, Ray Cornia, Jill Dahlberg,
  Marilyn Goff, Holly Hollingsworth, Susan Jorgensen,
  Barbara Milburn, Karmen Quinney, Cindy Stoeckl,
  Kim Taylor, Sara Toliver, Desirée Wybrow

If you have any questions or comments, please contact:
Chapelle, Ltd., Inc., P.O. Box 9252, Ogden, UT 84409
(801) 621-2777 • (801) 621-2788 Fax
e-mail: chapelle@chapelleltd.com
website: chapelleltd.com

Library of Congress Cataloging-in-Publication Data Available

10 9 8 7 6 5 4 3 2 1

Published by Sterling Publishing Co., Inc.
387 Park Avenue South, New York, NY 10016
Originally published in hardcover under the title
Tole-Painted Garden Furniture
©2002 by Chapelle Limited
Distributed in Canada by Sterling Publishing
c/o Canadian Manda Group, One Atlantic Avenue, Suite 105
Toronto, Ontario, Canada M6K 3E7
Distributed in Great Britain by Chryslis Books
64 Brewery Road, London N7 9NT, England
Distributed in Australia by Capricorn Link (Australia) Pty. Ltd.
P.O. Box 704, Windsor, NSW 2756, Australia
Printed in China
All Rights Reserved

Sterling ISBN 1-4027-0887-4

Dedication

I would like to thank Jo Packham, the ever-so-patient Cindy Stoeckl, and everyone at Chapelle for giving me the opportunity to do another book. It is a pleasure working with such a great group of people.

A special thanks to Desirée Wybrow for her endless hours of sanding, base-coating, and varnishing—and for being the greatest friend ever. I could not have made all the deadlines without your help.

I greatly appreciate my husband, Reed, for his patience, love, and understanding. He has kept the home fires burning while I have put in long hours to finish this book. He has always encouraged me to do the things I love and has been a great support. I love and appreciate you more than words can say.

I would like to dedicate this book to my mom and dad, Dee and Steve Larkin, for all their love, encouragement, and understanding and for helping me whenever needed all these years. I would especially like to thank my dad for making my projects so strong that they will last the test of time. You are the greatest parents ever.

Areta

Acknowledgments

The projects in this volume were created with outstanding and innovative products provided by the following manufacturers and retailers:

Delta Technical Coatings Inc.
2550 Pellissier Place
Whitter, CA 90601
telephone: (562) 695-7969
fax: (562) 695-5157
www.deltacrafts.com

Folk Art Brand Paints
Plaid Enterprises Inc.
3225 West Tech Drive
Norcross, GA 30092
telephone: (800) 842-4197
www.plaidonline.com

Aleene's
Duncan Enterprises
5673 Shields Ave.
Fresno, CA 93727
telephone: (559) 291-4444
fax: (559) 291-9444
email: consumer@duncanmail.com

Deco Art Americana
P.O. Box 327
Stanford, KY 40484
telephone: (606) 365-3193
telephone: (606) 365-9739

Black Gold Brushes
FM Brush Company
70-02 72nd Place
Glendale, NY 11385
fax: (718) 821-2385
email: info@fmbrush.com

Maxine's Mop Brushes
Loew Cornell
563 Chestnut Ave.
Teaneck, NJ 07666-2491
telephone: (201) 836-7070
telephone: (201) 836-8110
email: sales@loew-cornell.com

About the Author

I remember the first time I saw a tole-painted item. It was a beautiful teapot with fruit painted on it. Being somewhat skilled with crafts, I wanted very much to learn this painting technique. After extensive searching, I found a teacher and began a 23-year love affair with my new-found art form.

Since then, I have enjoyed teaching for various shops and conventions. I enjoyed owning my own craft shop—Country Pleasures. With my own designed pattern packets, I have traveled to all the major conventions to display and sell my creations. However, after all these years, I still have not painted a teapot for myself.

I live in Syracuse, Utah, with husband Reed, who has always been very supportive in all my creative endeavors. We are the proud parents of five sons.

For the past four years, I have been a designer for Chapelle, Ltd., doing the work I love.

Introduction

This book brings together more of Areta Bingham's inspired outdoor projects. Each piece of garden furniture—from potting table to patio table, planter to pedestal—began with a one-of-a-kind thrift store find.

These discarded pieces were given new life and purpose through the simple painting techniques and thoughtful use of color that typify Areta's realistic style and artistic sense of design.

Picking up where her first book, *Tole-Painted Outdoor Projects*, left off, this book is packed with a multitude of flowers, leaves, and outdoor elements to choose from. Although the surface preparation instructions may be specific to each found item, the possibilities are endless for combining designs and applying the painting techniques.

Painted Garden Furniture Projects is written for the reader who already has a general knowledge of tole-painting. Although these tole-painted projects are supported by step-by-step instructions, color worksheets, and detailed patterns, the techniques used to create them go beyond the basics and yield fabulous pieces that will rival the natural beauties of the garden.

Remember, no two artists work the same way and you should not expect to reproduce carbon copies of the projects in this book. Put your own personality, skill, and imagination into each project and create your own beautiful and unique treasures.

Contents

Introduction, 5

Supplies, 8

Basic Painting Techniques, 11

Surface Preparation, 15

Painting Tips, 16

Finishing, 17

Rustic Morning Glory Birdhouse, 18

Faux Tile Table, 23 & 36

Oversized Grapes Chair, 30

Oversized Strawberries Chair, 33

Geranium Planter, 40

Folk Art Tables, 45

Flowered Washstand Birdbath, 50

Hydrangea Door, 54

Angel Trumpet Potting Table, 57

Contents

Tulip Pedestal, 62

Second-hand Chic Table, 67

Autumn Leaves Hutch, 74

Berries & Vines Twig Shelves, 78

Gaillardia & Dahlia Washtubs, 82

Romantic Roses Bench, 89

Wood-burned Trout Table, 94

Poppies Bench, 100

Patio Storage Cabinet, 105

Paint Conversion Chart, 141

Metric Conversion Chart, 143

Index, 144

Supplies

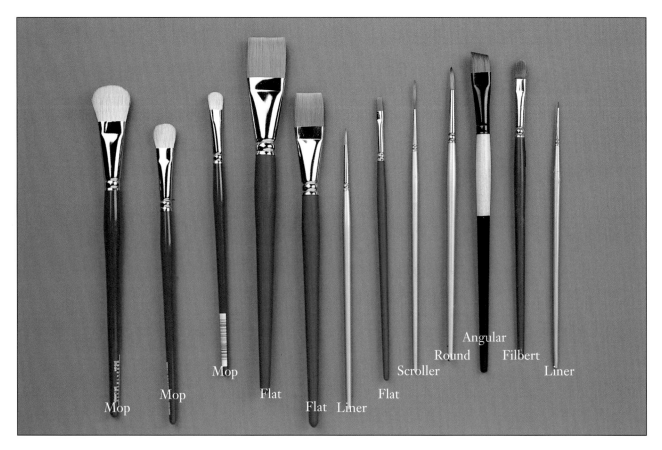

Many of the supplies necessary for the projects in this book may already be in your studio. Feel free to substitute paint colors and brands, paintbrush sizes, and other materials.

Paintbrushes

Use whatever paintbrush is most comfortable for you. Incorporate the largest brush possible for the area to be painted. Listed below are the paintbrushes used on projects in this book.

Angular paintbrushes: ⅜", ½"—used for floating

Filbert paintbrushes: #4, #6, #8, #10—used for stroking flower petals or tinting

Flat paintbrushes: #4, #6, #8, #10, #12— used for base-coating, floating, shading, and highlighting; ½" flat—used for applying retarder; 1" flat—used to apply varnish

Liner paintbrush: #1—used for small detailing

Mop paintbrush—used for blending and softening

Old flat scruffy paintbrush (not shown)—used for stippling and dry-brushing

Round paintbrushes: #3, #5—used for stroke work

Scroller or script paintbrushes: #5/0, #10/0— used for fine lines and detailing

Wash paintbrushes (not shown): ½", ¾", 1"— used for base-coating and floating large items

Paints

Acrylic paints are high-quality, bottled acrylic colors. Their rich, creamy formulation and long open time make them perfect for decorative painting. Cleanup is easy with soap and water.

Products from a number of respected paint companies were used when making the projects in this book. In each project supply list, the letter preceding the paint color represents which company makes the particular color used.

A = Americana
D = Delta
L = Aleene's
F = Folk Art (Plaid)

The Paint Conversion Chart on pages 141–143 lists the paints used throughout the book and converts them into other paint companies' color equivalents.

Miscellaneous Supplies

1. **Art eraser**—to remove pattern lines

2. **Black permanent marker**—to trace patterns

3. **Blow dryer**—to speed drying

4. **Disposable foam bowls and plates** (not shown)—for varnish and for mixing paints

5. **Exterior water-based varnish**—to protect projects

6. **Foam roller**—to apply paint or varnish

7. **Low-tack masking tape**—to secure patterns

8. **Palette** (not shown)—to arrange and mix paints

9. **Palette knife**—to mix paints

10. **Paper towels**—to wipe paintbrushes and clean up spills

11. **Retarder medium**—to slow down drying time

12. **Ruler**—to measure placement

13. **Sandpaper or sanding ovals** (various grits)— to remove rough spots from painting surfaces

14. **Sea sponge**—to sponge paint

15. **Sponge brushes**—to apply paint

16. **Stiff stencil brush or toothbrush**—to flyspeck

17. **Stylus** (not shown)—to transfer patterns and apply dots of paint

18. **Tack cloth**—to remove sanding dust from wood

19. **Tracing paper**—to trace patterns from book

20. **Transfer paper**—to transfer patterns onto surface

21. **Water container**—to rinse paintbrushes

22. **Wood filler**—to fill holes and gaps in wood

23. **Wood sealer**—to prepare surface before painting

(See individual project instructions for additional supplies needed.)

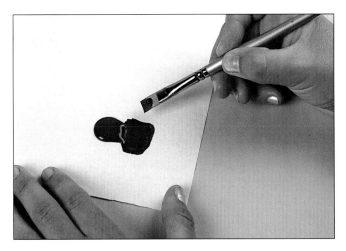

Load

Stroke paintbrush back and forth in paint until brush is full.

Double-load

Dip one side edge of lightly dampened flat paintbrush into paint, covering half the width of brush. Dip other side of brush into a different color. Stroke loaded brush on palette to soften color from side to side. Blend both sides of brush.

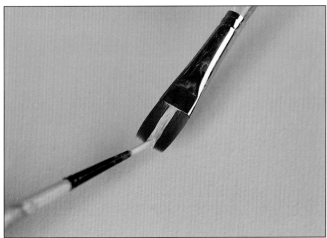

Side-load

Dip flat paintbrush into water, then touch to a paper towel until bristles lose their shine. Pull one side edge of paintbrush through puddle of paint. Stroke paintbrush in same place on palette until there is full-strength paint on one edge and clear water on the other.

Center-load

Dip flat paintbrush into water, then touch to a paper towel until bristles lose their shine. Load liner paintbrush with paint color to be floated. Paint a stripe onto center of flat paintbrush from the ferrel to its tip. Stroke center-loaded flat brush on palette to soften color. Paint should fade from center on each side of brush.

11

Base-coat

Cover an entire area with one initial coat. The paint must be smooth, without ridges or brush strokes. Start in center of project and paint out to edges to prevent ridges on edges. Project may require additional coats for opaque coverage.

Light coats of paint will prevent ridges in the overall area. A heavier coat of paint does not cover faster, it just looks messier. Leave base coat as background or shade and highlight on top of base coat.

Dry-brush

Using old flat scruffy paintbrush, pick up small amount of paint, then brush over paper towel to remove excess and work paint into bristles. Scrub over project where highlights are needed.

12

Wash

Mix paint with water until well blended. The more water used, the more transparent the color will be; the less water used the more opaque. Apply a wash of color, then let it dry. If project needs more color, apply another wash.

First Shade

Shading adds depth to painting. Side-load paintbrush and blend color on palette. The first shading color will establish shadow areas and create shape and contour. Outside edges can also be defined. The first shade color can also be repeated to create more depth.

Second Shade

Apply a darker value in areas that have already been shaded to deepen them. Keep second shading smaller than previous shading or work will be dark and muddy looking.

Third Shade

Sometimes a third value will be needed. This will be done like the second shade, but will cover an even smaller area and will only be applied where there was a second shading. It will be used to define the darkest recesses.

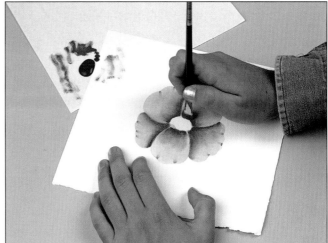

Shade or Highlight with Mop

Coat the surface with retarder medium. Side-load the shade color and float on shading. Mop the shadow out softly. Repeat until the desired results are achieved. Be certain to let area dry each time before proceeding. Use the same method when highlighting. Avoid using a wet paintbrush. Scrub mop paintbrush over a wet paper towel to remove most of previous color.

Highlight

Much like shading, load flat paintbrush with water then blot on paper towel. Side-load brush with highlight color, and apply to design. Two or three layers are usually required.

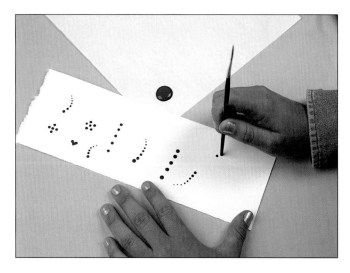

Dot

Make tiny dots by dipping the smaller end of a stylus or bristle tips of a scroller into paint, then touching the project. For bigger dots, use the end of any paintbrush handle. To make dots uniform, reload for every dot. For various sized dots, make as many dots as desired before reloading paint.

Tint

Tinting adds touches of color for interest and depth. The easiest way to tint an item is to use retarder medium.

Apply retarder medium to desired area. Load a small amount of paint on a filbert paintbrush and apply paint onto desired area. To soften color, lightly brush with a mop paintbrush to blend out. If not satisfied, paint will wipe right off so you

may start again. When complete, allow retarder medium and paint to dry. A hair dryer can be used to speed up the drying process. Let surface cool down before proceeding.

Repeat this process as often as necessary to get the desired effect.

Stipple

Pick up paint in the tips of the bristles of an old flat scruffy paintbrush. Tap bristles up and down on palette to remove excess and work paint into bristles, then tap on project.

Flyspeck

Load stiff-bristled paintbrush with paint mixed with water to the consistency of ink. Tap side of brush onto paper towel to remove excess paint. Hold brush with one hand over surface and, using a finger of the other hand, pull bristles in an upward motion so paint is flicked onto surface.

Scrolls or Fine Linework

Using a script, scroller, or liner paintbrush, fully load brush with paint mixed with water to the consistency of ink. Pull brush away from puddle of paint and roll brush slightly to make a nice point. There can be a lot of paint in the brush but not on the tip. If paint is the right consistency it will flow like ink.

A liner will not pull strokes as long as a scroller or script paintbrush because the bristles are not long enough to hold much paint. It is best to pull lines in flowers from the center out to the petals. Vein leaves from stem toward tip. Scrolls and tendrils are easier to do if you pull the brush toward you. Balance hand on little finger and forearm not just fingers.

Surface Preparation

Because so many of the pieces in this book were found items, the surface preparation technique used depended on the look desired for the piece. You will find that the techniques are not those traditionally applied when painting on an expensive piece of furniture. Use your own judgement and prepare the piece as much or as little as desired, depending on how the piece will be used. Just remember, the painting will only be as nice as the time taken to prepare the surface.

Rusted Metal

To paint over rusted metal, first prepare it by applying a rust-stopping primer, following manufacturer's instructions.

To remove rust prior to painting, apply a naval jelly, following manufacturer's instructions.

Galvanized Metal & Tin

Galvanized metal has an oily film that must be removed before painting. Using a moistened cloth, wash metal surface with a mixture of equal parts of vinegar and water, do not immerse piece in water. Allow to dry. Using fine (180–220 grit) sandpaper, sand lightly to roughen surface. Wipe with a tack cloth.

Spray surface with several light coats of metal primer, following manufacturer's instructions. Allow to dry 24 hours before proceeding.

Wood

If the wood is new and smooth, lightly sand the surface to create a tooth. Using a tack cloth, wipe off dust. Large wood pieces in bad condition may need to be sanded with a power sander. Wood that is old and weathered could be lightly sanded to make the paint flow better. Wood that has a peeling and cracked base coat needs to be lightly sanded to remove any loose paint.

In some cases, the existing finish may need to

be stripped. Use a product that is specific to the needs of your piece and follow the manufacturer's instructions. If the surface is too slick for the paint to stick, wash over the wood surface with a liquid sander/deglosser. Fill any undesirable nail holes and dents with wood filler. Allow to dry.

Follow directions for each individual piece to be painted. When base-coating, use as many coats as necessary to cover. Sand the final base coat with a brown paper bag.

Pattern Application

Many of the patterns for the projects in this book have been reduced in order to give the maximum number of projects and patterns possible. Percentages provided on patterns are for actual size of painted sample. Enlarge pattern on photocopier and adjust the size to accommodate the painting surface.

Using a black permanent marker, trace adjusted pattern onto tracing paper. Position tracing paper on painting surface and tape one edge with masking tape. If a pattern has open ends on one side, place this side along edge of surface. Slide transfer paper underneath tracing paper and lightly trace pattern lines with a stylus. Unless instructed otherwise, do not press stylus too hard or it will dent wood. After base-coating project, it may be necessary to retrace pattern detail.

Do not trace lines for scrolls or tendrils. It is much easier to freehand these items.

Painting Tips

Working with Acrylics

Squeeze paint onto palette, making a nickel-sized puddle of paint. Using paintbrush, pull color from edge of puddle. Avoid dipping brush in center of puddle, putting too much paint on edges. Allow each coat to dry before applying another coat.

16

Retarder Medium

Retarder medium is an additive used to ease the blending of colors and to extend drying time. Use a small container to hold the retarder medium as you paint. Designate a flat paintbrush for retarder medium only and keep it free from water. It will not damage the brush to keep it in retarder medium over extended periods. Rinse retarder medium from paintbrush when project is completed.

Dip a dry paintbrush into a small container of retarder medium; touch brush to a paper towel. Apply retarder medium onto area to be shaded, highlighted, or tinted. The area should look satiny, not wet and shiny. It is important not to use too much retarder medium or paint will run. Then apply paint colors as instructed.

Allow each painted area to dry before proceeding.

Yellow Glaze Medium

Transparent yellow pigment mixed in a clear glaze medium. This transparent color is chosen for its ability to impart a glowing quality without hazing. Lightly apply retarder medium onto painting area and work a little yellow glaze medium over highlights where desired.

Blue Glaze Medium

Similar to yellow glaze medium, this is a transparent blue pigment mixed in a clear glaze medium. Again, lightly apply retarder medium onto painting area and work a little blue glaze medium over highlights where desired.

Finishing

Using tack cloth, remove lint, dust, or dirt. Erase any remaining pattern lines.

Choose finishes that are nonyellowing and quick drying.

If project is made of new wood and was stained or glazed, the wood is rather porous. This means the surface will soak up most of the first coat of finish, requiring more coats than a painted surface.

Pieces that are used outdoors will need more finish coats applied periodically throughout the years.

Exterior Spray Varnish

Exterior spray varnishes are sprayed onto painted surfaces to seal and protect against moisture, soil, and dust. They are available in satin, matte, or gloss and dry clear without yellowing.

Exterior spray varnishes are convenient and easy to use for smaller projects. Spray the dry, completed project with a coat of varnish. Allow to dry. Spray a second coat and allow to dry. Sand surface with wet 400-grit sandpaper. Using a tack cloth, wipe away all dust. If necessary, apply an additional finish coat.

Exterior Water-based Varnish

Exterior water-based varnishes are brushed onto surfaces to seal and protect against moisture, soil, and dust. They come in satin, matte, or gloss finishes. They also offer excellent resistance to scratches and water spotting.

To achieve a soft finish on large items, apply exterior water-based varnish with a foam roller. Do not worry about bubbles, with repeated rollings the bubbles will vanish. Roll until varnish is near dry.

Materials

Painting Surface:
Wooden birdhouse: 11" x 20½"

Acrylic Paints:
D: Bahama Purple
D: Black
D: Dark Jungle
A: Hot Shots Thermal Green
D: Light Foliage
D: Medium Foliage
D: Purple
D: Rhythm 'N Blue
A: Royal Purple
D: White
A: Wisteria

Paintbrushes:
Assorted flats
Liner
Mop
Scroller
Small round
Soft-bristle: 2"

Supplies:
Disposable foam plates for
    varnish
Exterior water-based matte
    varnish
Palette
Palette knife
Paper towels
Retarder medium
Sandpaper
Stylus
Tack cloth
Water container
White transfer paper

I found this quaint birdhouse at a local handmade gift boutique. I had many ideas for painting on it, but settled on the morning glory.

Instructions

Surface Preparation:

1. Refer to Surface Preparation on pages 15–16.

2. Lightly sand rough areas for a better painting surface. Using tack cloth, wipe off any sawdust.

3. Determine placement of motifs, then transfer main pattern lines of Rustic Morning Glory Birdhouse Patterns on pages 114–115 onto surface.

Paint:

1. Refer to Basic Painting Techniques on pages 11–15.

Morning Glories

1. Refer to Morning Glory & Bud Worksheet on page 20. Using flat paintbrush, base-coat all morning glories and buds with Wisteria.

2. Transfer remaining pattern lines onto surface, going over base-coated morning glories for petal definition.

3. Using flat paintbrush, apply retarder medium onto one morning glory or bud at a time. Using flat paintbrush, shade morning glory or bud with very wide float of Bahama Purple. Soften, using a mop paintbrush. Repeat for each morning glory and bud.

4. Using flat paintbrush, apply retarder medium onto one morning glory or bud at a time. Using flat paintbrush, shade morning glory or bud with Rhythm 'N Blue, taking care to avoid covering all the previously floated color. Soften, using a mop paintbrush. Repeat for each morning glory and bud.

5. Using flat paintbrush, apply retarder medium onto one morning glory or bud at a time. Using flat paintbrush, shade morning glory

(continued on page 21)

Morning Glory & Bud Worksheet

1. Base-coat and shade.

2. 2nd shade.

3. 3rd shade.

4. Highlight.

5. Add calyx.

6. Shade and highlight calyx. Tint bud.

1. Base-coat and shade.

2. 2nd shade.

3. 3rd shade.

4. Highlight.

5. Add lines. Shade throat.

6. 2nd throat shade. Add strokes to center of throat. Shade and highlight throat. Paint, shade and highlight calyx. Tint as desired.

(continued from page 18)

or bud with Purple. Soften, using a mop paintbrush. Repeat as needed. Note: Do not float every previously shaded area with Purple. It should be applied in a random fashion to areas that need to be darkened.

6. Using flat paintbrush, apply retarder medium onto one morning glory or bud at a time. Using flat paintbrush, highlight morning glory or bud with Wisteria. Soften, using a mop paintbrush. Repeat for each morning glory and bud. Note: For a stronger highlight, mix Wisteria + a little White.

7. Using flat paintbrush, apply retarder medium onto one morning glory at a time. Using flat paintbrush, highlight morning glory with a center-loaded float of Wisteria. Repeat for each morning glory. Soften, using a mop paintbrush.

8. Using liner paintbrush, line morning glories with Wisteria. Note: If needed, add a little White.

9. Using flat paintbrush, float throat of morning glories with Light Foliage. Using liner paintbrush, paint center strokes with Medium Foliage. Using liner paintbrush, create a shade on bottom of each stroke with Purple. Using liner paintbrush, create a highlight on top of each stroke with Light Foliage + a little White.

10. Using flat paintbrush, randomly float morning glories

with Royal Purple to add interest and color.

11. Using small round paintbrush, paint a calyx on all morning glories and buds with Medium Foliage. Using scroller paintbrush, stroke in all stems on morning glories and buds with Medium Foliage.

12. Using flat paintbrush, shade calyx with Dark Jungle.

13. Using flat paintbrush, highlight calyx with Light Foliage.

Leaves

1. Refer to Morning Glory Leaf Worksheet at right. Using flat paintbrush, base-coat all leaves with Medium Foliage. Using scroller paintbrush, stroke in all stems with Medium Foliage.

2. Using flat paintbrush, apply retarder medium onto one leaf at a time. Using flat paintbrush, shade bottom or left side of leaf with Dark Jungle. Shade center of leaf with Dark Jungle to indicate vein. Soften, using a mop paintbrush. Repeat for each leaf. Shade stems with Dark Jungle.

3. Using flat paintbrush, apply retarder medium onto one leaf at a time. Using flat paintbrush, highlight leaf with Light Foliage. Soften, using a mop paintbrush. Repeat for each leaf. Highlight stems with Light Foliage.

4. Using flat paintbrush, apply retarder medium onto one leaf at a time. Using flat paintbrush, shade leaf as needed with Dark Jungle + a little Black. Soften, using a mop paintbrush. Repeat for each leaf.

5. Using flat paintbrush, randomly float leaves with Hot Shots Thermal Green to accent highlight float.

6. Using flat paintbrush, apply retarder medium onto one leaf at a time. Using flat paintbrush, randomly tint leaf with any of the flower colors. Soften, using a mop paintbrush. Repeat for each leaf.

7. Using liner paintbrush, vein leaves with Medium Foliage + a little White.

Tendrils

1. Using scroller paintbrush, paint tendrils with Dark Jungle + a little Black.

Finish:

1. Using 2" soft-bristle paintbrush, apply three coats exterior water-based matte varnish, following manufacturer's instructions.

1. Base-coat and shade.

2. Highlight.

3. 2nd highlight.

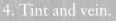

4. Tint and vein.

Materials

Painting Surface:
Old table: 35½" x 19½"

Acrylic Paints:
D: Autumn Brown
D: Black
D: Black Cherry
A: Black Forest Green
F: Butterscotch
A: Cadmium Orange
A: Cadmium Yellow
D: Chocolate Cherry
F: Crimson
L: Deep Blush
L: Deep Sage
D: Eucalyptus
A: Evergreen
F: Green Forest
A: Hot Shots Fiery Red
A: Hot Shots Red
A: Hot Shots Scorching
    Yellow
D: Leaf Green
A: Light Buttermilk
L: Light Lime
L: Medium Lime
L: Medium Turquoise
A: Mink Tan
A: Moon Yellow
F: Payne's Grey
F: Purple
D: Royal Plum
A: Sand
A: Snow White
L: True Red
D: White
A: Wisteria

Paintbrushes:
Assorted flats
Large mop
Liner
Old flat scruffy
Scroller
Small round
Soft-bristle: 3"
Stencil

Supplies:
Disposable foam plates
    for varnish
Exterior water-based
    gloss varnish
Grout tape: ¼"
Liquid sander/deglosser
Palette
Palette knife
Paper towels
Power sander and sand-
    paper
Retarder medium
Ruler
Soap
Small foam roller
Stain glazes: blue; yellow
    oxide
Stylus
Tack cloth
Towel
Water container
White transfer paper

This table, found at a local swap meet, is painted with tiles and fruits. I couldn't decide whether to make the fruits large or small, so I did the table twice—once with the large fruits and once with the small fruits.

Tile Instructions

See photo on page 23.

Surface Preparation:
1. Refer to Surface Preparation on pages 15–16.

2. Wash thoroughly with soap and water. Using a towel, dry surface.

3. Using power sander, lightly sand the painting area for a better painting surface. Using tack cloth, wipe off any dust.

4. Using liquid sander/deglosser, wash over painting area.

Paint:
1. Refer to Basic Painting Techniques on pages 11–15.

Tiles
1. Using small foam roller, base-coat table with Sand.

2. Determine what size tile would best suit your table by measuring its width and length. (Tiles shown are 5" x 5" while the small tiles around the edges are 2¼" x 1¼".) Tape off all tiles with grout tape. Note: Allow for ¼" grout space around tiles when measuring.

3. Refer to Tile Legend on opposite page. Using flat paintbrush, base-coat center portion of tile with light color. Hint: To slow drying time, mix retarder medium into paints.

4. Using flat paintbrush, base-coat around light color and to edge of tile with darker color.

5. Using large mop paintbrush, pounce over surface to soften and blend colors into each other. Note: Apply varied color combinations to simulate different colored tiles:

Tile Legend

Tile #1:   Center: Evergreen
             Around: Green Forest

Tile #2:   Center: Medium Lime
             Around: Green Forest

Tile #3:   Center: Medium
                    Turquoise
             Around: Green Forest

Tile #4:   Center: Deep Sage
             Around: Medium
                    Turquoise

Tile #5:   Center: Light Buttermilk
             Around: Medium
                    Turquoise

Tile #6:   Center: Medium Lime
             Around: Medium
                    Turquoise

Tile #7:   Center: Light Buttermilk
             Around: Medium Lime

Tile #8:   Center: Light Lime
             Around: Medium
                    Turquoise

Tile #9:   Center: Light Buttermilk
             Around: Deep Sage

Tile #10:   Center: Medium
                     Turquoise
              Around: Evergreen

6. Mix a wash of Greens and Turquoise. Apply washes over grout to soften color.

7. Using flat paintbrush, paint table legs with Green Forest.

8. Mix a wash of Deep Sage. Using flat paintbrush, apply wash over table legs.

9. Determine placement of fruits, then transfer Faux Tile Table Large Fruit Patterns on page 116 or Faux Tile Table Small Fruit Patterns on page 119 onto surface within tiles.

Large Apple Worksheet

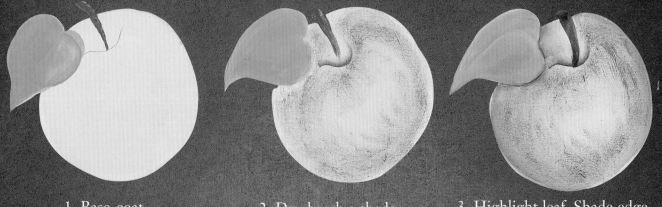

1. Base-coat.

2. Dry-brush a shade. Shade indentation for stem.

3. Highlight leaf. Shade edge of apple and behind leaf.

4. Shade leaf. Shade stem. Dry-brush a highlight.

5. Dry-brush a shade. Shade stem. Apply washes.

Large Fruit Instructions

Paint:
1. Refer to Basic Painting Techniques on pages 11–15.

Large Apple
1. Refer to Large Apple Worksheet above. Using flat paintbrush, base-coat apple with Moon Yellow.

2. Using flat paintbrush, base-coat leaf with Leaf Green.

3. Using small round paintbrush, base-coat stem with Autumn Brown.

4. Using old flat scruffy paintbrush, dry-brush a shade onto apple with Crimson.

5. Using flat paintbrush, shade indentation for stem with Crimson.

6. Using flat paintbrush, highlight leaf with Cadmium Yellow.

7. Using flat paintbrush, shade edge of apple and behind leaf with Crimson.

Large Plum Worksheet

1. Base-coat.

2. Dry-brush a highlight on plum. Highlight leaf.

3. Highlight top of plum. Shade crease of plum. Shade leaf.

4. Apply wash.

8. Using flat paintbrush, shade leaf with Black Forest Green.

9. Using flat paintbrush, shade stem with Payne's Grey.

10. Using old flat scruffy paintbrush, dry-brush a highlight onto apple with Snow White.

11. Using old flat scruffy paintbrush, dry-brush a shade onto apple with Crimson.

12. Using flat paintbrush, shade stem with Black Cherry.

13. Mix a wash of Black Cherry. Using flat paintbrush, apply wash around outside edge of apple.

14. Mix a wash of Cadmium Yellow. Using flat paintbrush, apply wash over entire apple for a golden look.

Large Plum

1. Refer to Large Plum Worksheet above. Using flat paintbrush, base-coat plum with Royal Plum.

2. Using flat paintbrush, base-coat leaf with Leaf Green.

3. Using old flat scruffy paintbrush, dry-brush a highlight onto plum with Wisteria.

4. Using flat paintbrush, highlight leaf with Cadmium Yellow.

5. Using small round paintbrush, base-coat stem with Autumn Brown.

6. Using flat paintbrush, highlight top of plum with Wisteria.

7. Using flat paintbrush, shade crease of plum with Royal Plum + a little Black.

8. Using flat paintbrush, shade leaf with Black Forest Green.

9. Mix a wash of Royal Plum. Using flat paintbrush, apply wash over leaf.

10. Using flat paintbrush, strengthen shade on crease of plum with Royal Plum + a little Black.

Large Pear Worksheet

1. Base-coat.

2. Dry-brush a highlight on pear.
Highlight leaf. Base-coat stem.

3. Dry-brush a shade
on pear.
Shade leaf.

4. Highlight pear.
Shade pear and leaf.

Large Cherry Worksheet

1. Base-coat.

2. Dry-brush a
highlight on cherry.
Highlight leaf.

3. Shade edge of
cherry. Shade leaf.

4. Highlight top
of cherry.

5. Apply wash.

Large Pear

1. Refer to Large Pear Worksheet on opposite page. Using flat paintbrush, base-coat pear with Moon Yellow.

2. Using flat paintbrush, base-coat leaf with Leaf Green.

3. Using old flat scruffy paintbrush, dry-brush a highlight onto pear with Snow White + Cadmium Yellow.

4. Using flat paintbrush, highlight leaf with Cadmium Yellow.

5. Using small round paintbrush, base-coat stem with Autumn Brown.

6. Using old flat scruffy paintbrush, dry-brush a shade onto pear with Deep Blush + Cadmium Orange.

7. Using flat paintbrush, highlight pear with Cadmium Yellow.

8. Using flat paintbrush, shade pear and leaf with Hot Shots Fiery Red.

9. Using flat paintbrush, shade leaf with Black Forest Green.

Large Cherries

1. Refer to Large Cherry Worksheet on opposite page. Using flat paintbrush, base-coat cherries with Crimson.

2. Using flat paintbrush, base-coat leaf with Leaf Green.

3. Using old flat scruffy paintbrush, dry-brush a highlight onto cherries with Snow White.

4. Using flat paintbrush, highlight leaf with Cadmium Yellow.

5. Using small round paintbrush, base-coat stems with Autumn Brown.

6. Using flat paintbrush, shade around edges of cherries and indentations for stems with Chocolate Cherry.

7. Using flat paintbrush, highlight tops of cherries with Cadmium Yellow + Snow White.

8. Using flat paintbrush, shade leaf with Black Forest Green.

9. Mix a wash of Hot Shots Fiery Red. Using flat paintbrush, apply wash over cherries.

Oversized Grapes Chair

Materials

Painting Surface:
Chair: 15" x 12" seat

Acrylic Paints:
A: Bittersweet Chocolate
D: Black
A: Black Green
A: Black Plum
A: Cadmium Orange
L: Deep Sage
D: G.P. Purple
D: Leaf green
L: Medium Lime
F: Medium Yellow
D: Vintage Wine

Paintbrushes:
Angular: ½"
Assorted flats
Liner
Old flat scruffy
Soft-bristle: 2"

Supplies:
Black transfer paper
Disposable foam plates for
    varnish
Exterior water-based satin
    varnish
Palette
Palette knife
Paper towels
Sandpaper
Stylus
Tack cloth
Water container

Tole painting is a great way to give new life to old patio furniture—like this weathered slat chair. A large cluster of purple grapes coordinates perfectly with the large fruit motifs on the Faux Tile Table featured on page 24.

Instructions

Designed by: Yvonne Heiner
Refer to photos on pages 23 and 32.

Note: When making each wash, use one part paint to two parts water.

Surface Preparation:
1. Refer to Surface Preparation on pages 15–16.

2. Lightly sand surface to prepare it to be painted. Using tack cloth, wipe off any sawdust.

3. Using flat paintbrush, base-coat chair with Deep Sage.

4. Mix a wash of Medium Lime. Using flat paintbrush, apply wash onto chair.

5. Determine placement of motifs, then transfer Oversized Grapes Chair Pattern on page 117 onto surface. Note: To transfer the pattern onto a slatted chair, cut the pattern into strips the same width as the slats and then transfer each strip in its correct order.

Paint:
1. Refer to Basic Painting Techniques on pages 11–15.

Grapes
1. Refer to Grapes Worksheet on opposite page. Using flat paintbrush, base-coat grapes with Cadmium Orange for an undercoat.

2. Using flat paintbrush, base-coat grapes with Vintage Wine.

3. Using flat paintbrush, base-coat stem with Bittersweet Chocolate.

4. Using old flat scruffy paintbrush, dry-brush a highlight on grapes with G.P. Purple.

(continued on page 32)

Grapes
Worksheet

Grape Leaf Worksheet

1. Base-coat.

1. Base-coat.

2. Highlight.

2. Highlight.

3. Shade.

3. Shade.

31

(continued from page 30)

5. Using flat paint-brush, highlight top of each grape with G.P. Purple.

6. Using flat paint-brush and starting at the top of each grape, shade all grapes with Black Plum.

7. Using flat paint-brush, shade along bottom of stem with Black.

Leaves & Vines

1. Refer to Grape Leaf Worksheet on page 31. Using flat paintbrush, base-coat all leaves and stems with Leaf Green.

2. Using flat paint-brush, shade dark recesses and vein lines in each leaf with Black Green.

3. Using flat paint-brush, highlight all light areas and vein lines with Medium Yellow.

4. Using liner paint-brush, stroke on some tendrils with Black Green.

Finish:

1. Using 2" soft-bristle paintbrush, apply three coats exterior water-based satin varnish, following manufacturer's instructions.

Materials

Painting Surface:
Chair: 15" x 12" seat

Acrylic Paints:
A: Bittersweet Chocolate
A: Black Green
A: Black Plum
A: Cadmium Orange
A: Cadmium Yellow
F: Crimson
A: Golden Straw
D: Leaf Green
L: Medium Lime
L: Medium Turquoise
F: Medium Yellow
A: Snow White

Paintbrushes:
Angular: ½"
Assorted flats
Liner
Old flat scruffy
Soft-bristle: 2"

Supplies:
Adhesive
Black transfer paper
Disposable foam plates for
    varnish
Exterior water-based satin
    varnish
Palette
Palette knife
Paper towels
Sandpaper
Silver foiling
Stylus
Tack cloth
Water container

Here is another design done on an old slat chair meant to accompany the Faux Tile Table with large fruit featured on page 24. These strawberries look so true to life, one would hesitate to sit on them!

Instructions

Designed by: Yvonne Heiner
Refer to photos on pages 23 and 35.

Note: When making each wash, use one part paint to two parts water.

Surface Preparation:
1. Refer to Surface Preparation on pages 15–16.

2. Lightly sand surface to prepare it to be painted. Using tack cloth, wipe off any sawdust.

3. Using flat paintbrush, base-coat chair with Medium Turquoise.

4. Apply two coats of adhesive onto chair. Allow to dry 24 hours. Apply foiling onto chair, following manufacturer's instructions.

5. Mix a wash of Medium Lime. Using flat paintbrush, apply wash onto chair.

6. Determine placement of motifs, then transfer Oversized Strawberries Chair Pattern on page 118 onto surface. Note: To transfer the pattern onto a slatted chair, cut the pattern into strips the same width as the slats and then transfer each strip in its correct order.

Paint:
1. Refer to Basic Painting Techniques on pages 11–15.

Strawberries
1. Refer to Strawberry Worksheet on page 34. Using flat paintbrush, base-coat strawberries with Snow White for an undercoat.

2. Using flat paintbrush, base-coat strawberries with Cadmium Orange and calyxes with Leaf Green.

Strawberry Worksheet

1. Base-coat.

2. Dry-brush a highlight on strawberries.

3. Shade calyx. Stroke on seeds. Stroke a shade on seeds.

4. Shade strawberry.

5. Shade under calyx.

6. Highlight.

3. Using old flat scruffy paintbrush, dry-brush a highlight on center of each strawberry with Snow White.

4. Using flat paintbrush, shade calyxes with Black Green.

5. Using liner paintbrush, stroke on seeds with Golden Straw.

6. Using liner paintbrush, paint another little stroke just to the side of each seed with Bittersweet Chocolate.

7. Using flat paintbrush, shade strawberries with Crimson.

8. Using flat paintbrush, shade strawberries under the calyxes with Black Plum.

9. Using flat paintbrush, highlight strawberries with Cadmium Yellow.

10. Mix a wash of Crimson. Using flat paintbrush, apply wash onto strawberries.

Strawberry Leaf Worksheet

1. Base-coat.

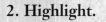

2. Highlight.

3. Shade.

Leaves & Vines

1. Refer to Strawberry Leaf Worksheet at left. Using flat paintbrush, base-coat all leaves and stems with Leaf Green.

2. Using flat paintbrush, shade dark recesses and behind any leaf that is behind another with Black Green.

3. Using flat paintbrush, highlight all light areas with Medium Yellow.

4. Using liner paintbrush, pull on some tendrils with thinned Black Green.

Finish:

1. Using 2" soft-bristle paintbrush, apply three coats exterior water-based satin varnish, following manufacturer's instructions.

Small Fruit Instructions

This is an alternate way for painting the Faux Tile Table with smaller versions of the fruits.

Paint:

1. Refer to Materials and Tile Instructions on pages 24–25. Refer to Basic Painting Techniques on pages 11–15.

Small Apple

1. Refer to Small Apple Worksheet on opposite page. Using flat paintbrush, base-coat apple with Moon Yellow.

2. Using flat paintbrush, shade apple with True Red.

3. Using flat paintbrush, highlight apple with Medium Lime.

4. Using stencil paintbrush flyspeck apple with Butterscotch.

5. Using flat paintbrush, strengthen shades or highlights as needed.

6. Using small round paintbrush, base-coat stem with Autumn Brown.

7. Using flat paintbrush, shade stem with Autumn Brown + Black.

8. Using flat paintbrush, highlight stem with Mink Tan.

9. Using flat paintbrush, base-coat leaf with Eucalyptus.

10. Using flat paintbrush, apply retarder medium onto leaf. Using flat paintbrush, shade leaf with Green Forest.

11. Using flat paintbrush, apply retarder medium onto leaf. Using flat paintbrush, highlight leaf with Medium Lime.

12. Using flat paintbrush, apply retarder medium onto leaf. Using flat paintbrush, tint leaf with True Red.

13. Using flat paintbrush, float behind apple, leaf, and stem with Green Forest.

Small Apple Worksheet

1. Base-coat and shade.

2. Highlight.

3. Flyspeck.

4. Strengthen shades and highlights.

5. Base-coat, shade, and highlight stem. Base-coat, shade, highlight, and tint leaf.

Small Pear
1. Refer to Small Pear Worksheet on page 38. Using flat paintbrush, base-coat pear with Moon Yellow.

2. Using flat paintbrush, paint pear with yellow oxide glaze.

3. Using flat paintbrush, highlight pear with Hot Shots Scorching Yellow. Soften, using mop paintbrush.

4. Using flat paintbrush, shade pear with True Red. Soften, using mop paintbrush.

5. Using flat paintbrush, paint a highlight stroke with White.

6. Repeat Steps 6–12 for Small Apple on opposite page to paint stem and leaf.

7. Using flat paintbrush, float behind pear, leaf, and stem with Green Forest.

Small Cherries
1. Refer to Small Cherry Worksheet on page 38. Using flat paintbrush, base-coat cherries with True Red.

2. Using flat paintbrush, shade cherries with Chocolate Cherry + True Red.

3. Using a flat paintbrush, highlight cherries with Hot Shots Red.

4. Using liner paintbrush, paint highlight strokes with White.

5. Repeat Steps 6–12 for Small Apple on opposite page to paint stems and leaves.

(continued on page 39)

Small Pear Worksheet

1. Base-coat.

2. Glaze.

3. Highlight.

4. Shade.

5. Highlight strokes to pear. Base-coat, shade, and highlight stem. Base-coat, shade, highlight, and tint leaves.

Small Cherry Worksheet

1. Base-coat and shade.

2. Highlight.

3. Glaze.
4. Strengthen shade.
5. Base-coat, shade, and highlight stem. Add highlight stroke to plum.

Small Plum Worksheet

1. Base-coat and shade.

2. Highlight.

3. Glaze. Strengthen shade.

4. Base-coat, shade, and highlight stem. Add highlight stroke to plum. Base-coat, shade, highlight, and tint leaf.

(continued from page 37)

6. Using flat paintbrush, shade behind cherries, leaves, and stems with Green Forest.

7. Using scroller paintbrush, paint tendrils with Green Forest.

Small Plums

1. Refer to Small Plum Worksheet above. Using flat paintbrush, base-coat plums with Purple.

2. Using flat paintbrush, shade plums with Purple + Black.

3. Using flat paintbrush, highlight plums with Purple + White.

4. Using flat paintbrush, paint over plums with blue stain glaze.

5. Using flat paintbrush, strengthen shade with Purple + Black.

6. Using flat paintbrush, paint highlight strokes with White.

7. Repeat Steps 6–11 for Small Apple on page 36 to paint stem and leaf.

8. Using flat paintbrush, tint leaf with Purple.

9. Using flat paintbrush, float behind plums, leaf, and stem with Deep Sage.

Finish:

1. Using 3" soft-bristle paintbrush, apply three coats exterior water-based gloss varnish, following manufacturer's instructions.

Materials

Painting Surfaces:
Enamelware cooking pot:
  14" dia. x 10" high
Wrought-iron barstool base

Acrylic Paints:
D: Black
F: Butterscotch
D: Dark Jungle
D: Eucalyptus
F: Green Forest
A: Hot Shots Sizzling Pink
L: Medium Turquoise
A: Napa Red
A: Olive Green
L: True Red

Paintbrushes:
Assorted flats
Liner
Mop
Round

Supplies:
Bolts: ¼" x 1" (4)
Exterior spray paint: red
Exterior spray primer
Exterior satin spray varnish
Hammer
Palette
Palette knife
Paper towels
Power drill and drill bits:
  ⅛"; ¼"
Retarder medium
Screwdrivers: flathead;
  phillips
Soap
Stylus
Towel
Water-based metal primer
Water container
White transfer paper
Wing nuts: ¼" (4)

While shopping at a thrift store, I saw this wonderful pot trimmed in red. At the time, I didn't know what I was going to do with it, but I had to have it. Six months later, I found a wrought-iron barstool that would make a great stand for my pot. Together, they make a perfect planter for geraniums.

Instructions

Surface Preparation:

1. Refer to Surface Preparation on pages 15–16.

2. If seat is intact, remove from barstool and discard. There should be four holes in the base where the seat was attached. Turn pot upside down and set barstool on top of it. Position phillips screwdriver in hole of barstool. Using hammer, tap lightly to mark where holes need to be. Set barstool aside.

3. Using power drill, drill four ¼" holes in bottom of pot to fit bolts. Randomly drill several ⅛" holes in bottom of pot for drainage.

4. If barstool is in good condition, wash surface thoroughly with soap and water. Using a towel, dry surface. If it has peeling paint or rust, you will need to prepare it, following general instructions for Rusted Metal on page 15.

5. Apply several light coats exterior spray primer onto barstool, following manufacturer's instructions, until well covered. Allow to dry 24 hours.

6. Apply several coats red exterior spray paint, following manufacturer's instructions. Allow to dry.

7. Wash pot thoroughly with soap and water. Allow to dry. Using flat paintbrush, apply water-based metal primer onto outside of pot, following manufacturer's instructions. Allow to dry 24 hours.

8. Determine placement of motifs, then transfer Geranium Planter Pattern on page 120 onto surface.

Paint:

1. Refer to Basic Painting Techniques on pages 11–15.

1. Base-coat.

2. Shade petals and buds.

3. Line petals.

4. Highlight petals and buds.

5. Add specks to centers.

Geraniums & Buds

1. Refer to Geranium & Bud Worksheet above. Using flat paintbrush, base-coat all bud calyx with Eucalyptus until opaque for an undercoat.

2. Using flat paintbrush, base-coat all geraniums and bud flowering tips with True Red.

3. Using flat paintbrush, shade behind top geraniums and petals with Napa Red. Shade behind where one petal overlaps another with Napa Red. Using liner paintbrush, line all petals with Napa Red. Using flat paintbrush, shade all buds at the base with Napa Red.

4. Using flat paintbrush, highlight all petals and buds with Hot Shots Sizzling Pink.

5. Using liner paintbrush, paint specks on geranium centers with Butterscotch.

6. Using flat paintbrush, shade base of buds and behind each section of unopened large bud with Green Forest. Shade stems.

7. Using flat paintbrush, highlight bud ends and stems with Olive Green.

Geranium Leaf & Pod Worksheet

1. Base-coat.

2. Shade.

3. Highlight.

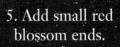

4. Strengthen
shade if
necessary.

5. Add small red
blossom ends.

1. Undercoat.

2. Base-coat and shade.

3. Highlight.

4. Add line of red
and soften.

5. Tint. Darken any
shading if needed.

43

Leaves & Pods

1. Refer to Geranium Leaf & Pod Worksheet on page 43. Using flat paintbrush, base-coat all leaves, stems, and pod with Eucalyptus until opaque for an undercoat.

2. Using flat paintbrush, base-coat all leaves, stems, and pod with Dark Jungle.

3. Using flat paintbrush, apply retarder medium onto one leaf at a time. Using flat paintbrush, shade where one leaf overlaps another with Green Forest. Shade creases in leaf to indicate veins with Green Forest. Soften, using a mop paintbrush. Repeat for each leaf.

4. Using flat paintbrush, apply retarder medium onto one leaf at a time. Using flat paintbrush, highlight leaf with Olive Green. Soften, using a mop paintbrush. Repeat for each leaf.

5. Using flat paintbrush, apply retarder medium onto one leaf at a time. Using round paintbrush, paint a line around perimeter of and centered within leaf with True Red. Soften edges, using a mop paintbrush. Repeat for each leaf.

6. Using flat paintbrush, apply retarder medium onto one leaf at a time. Using flat paintbrush, tint leaf with Medium Turquoise. Soften, using a mop paintbrush. Repeat for each leaf.

7. Using flat paintbrush, apply retarder medium onto one leaf at a time. Using flat paintbrush, shade where dimension is needed with Green Forest + a little Black. Soften, using a mop paintbrush. Repeat for each leaf.

Finish:

1. Apply three coats exterior satin spray varnish, following manufacturer's instructions.

Assembly:

1. Place pot on top of barstool, aligning holes. Insert ¼" x 1" bolts through bottom of barstool and into pot. Fasten with wing nuts to hold pot in place.

Materials

Painting Surfaces:
Wooden end tables:
  15¾" square x 2' high (2)

Acrylic Paints:
D: Autumn Brown
D: Black Cherry
D: Burnt Sienna
A: Deep Burgundy
A: Driftwood
A: Mauve
D: White

Paintbrushes:
Assorted flats
Chip: 2" (5)

Supplies:
Black transfer paper
Clean soft rags
Disposable foam bowls for
  mixing paint
Exterior satin spray varnish
Liquid sander/deglosser
Palette
Palette knife
Paper towels
Sandpaper
Soap
Stylus
Tack cloth
Towel
Water container
Water-based glaze medium

I found these tables at a flea market. They were very stable and the paint was cracked and peeling. Here, I could actually purchase what painters often try to duplicate with a paint finish. What a great project—just waiting to be painted.

Instructions

See photo on page 45.

Note: When making each wash, use one part paint to two parts water.

Surface Preparation:

For Antiqued Finish
1. Refer to Surface Preparation on pages 15–16.

2. Lightly sand off any loose or peeling paint for a better painting surface. Using tack cloth, wipe off any dust.

3. Wash surface thoroughly with soap and water. Using a towel, dry surface.

4. Using liquid sander/deglosser, wash over painting area.

5. Determine placement of motifs, then transfer Folk Art Tables Pattern on page 121 onto surface.

For Faux Finish
1. In disposable bowl, mix one part paint to two parts glaze medium for each of the following colors: Black Cherry, Burnt Sienna, Deep Burgundy, Driftwood, Mauve, and White.

2. Using chip paintbrush, create crisscross strokes with Burnt Sienna mixture, taking care to avoid covering entire area.

3. Using chip paintbrush and working quickly, randomly apply Driftwood mixture between Burnt Sienna strokes, allowing some of the colors to overlap. Soften colors and blend any brush marks, using a clean soft rag.

4. Using chip paintbrush, randomly apply White mixture over

previously painted colors. Soften colors and blend any brush marks, using a clean soft rag.

5. Using chip paintbrush, apply Black Cherry, Deep Burgundy, and Mauve mixtures over previously painted colors. Soften colors, using a clean soft rag until glazes are mottled.

6. Determine placement of motifs, then transfer Folk Art Tables Pattern on page 121 onto surface.

Paint:

1. Refer to Basic Painting Techniques on pages 11–15.

Florals on Antiqued Finish

1. Refer to Florals on Antiqued Finish Worksheet on page 48. Using flat paintbrush, base-coat all motifs with Mauve + a little White.

2. Using flat paintbrush, shade all motifs with Deep Burgundy.

3. Mix a wash of Autumn Brown. Using flat paintbrush, apply wash onto entire design so that it soaks down into the cracks and to soften paint colors. Using paper towel, wipe off excess.

Florals on Faux Finish

1. Refer to Florals on Faux Finish Worksheet on page 49. Using flat paintbrush, base-coat all motifs with Mauve + White.

2. Using flat paintbrush, shade all motifs with Autumn Brown.

Finish:

1. Apply three coats exterior satin spray varnish, following manufacturer's instructions.

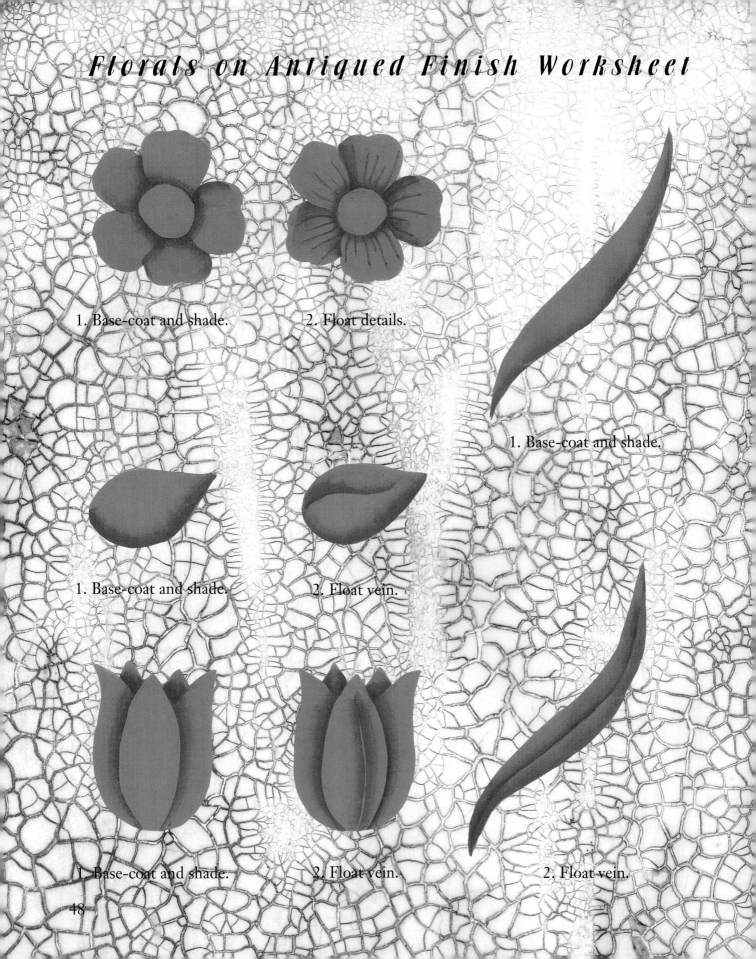

Florals on Antiqued Finish Worksheet

1. Base-coat and shade.

2. Float details.

1. Base-coat and shade.

1. Base-coat and shade.

2. Float vein.

1. Base-coat and shade.

2. Float vein.

2. Float vein.

48

Florals on Faux Finish Worksheet

1. Base-coat and shade.

2. Float details.

1. Base-coat and shade.

1. Base-coat and shade.

2. Float vein.

1. Base-coat and shade.

2. Float vein.

2. Float vein.

Materials

Painting Surface:
Old metal washstand:
  24" x 19" x 30" high

Acrylic Paints:
A: Antique Rose
A: Arbor Green
A: Gooseberry Pink
F: Green Forest
A: Honey Brown
A: Mint Julep Green
A: Moon Yellow
D: Red Iron Oxide
D: White

Paintbrushes:
Assorted flats
Liner
Scroller

Supplies:
Black transfer paper
Exterior satin spray varnish
Palette
Palette knife
Paper towels
Soap
Stylus
Towel
Water container
Water-based metal primer

What a find! An old washstand—complete with the bowl. I could hardly wait to put my paintbrush to its surface.

Instructions

Surface Preparation:

1. Refer to Surface Preparation on pages 15–16.

2. Wash surface thoroughly with soap and water. Using a towel, dry surface.

3. Apply a coat of water-based metal primer, following manufacturer's instructions. Allow to dry.

4. Determine placement of motifs, then transfer Flowered Washstand Birdbath Patterns on page 122 onto surface.

Paint:
1. Refer to Basic Painting Techniques on pages 11–15.

Innermost Flower Leaves

1. Refer to Flower Leaf Worksheet below. Using flat paintbrush, base-coat innermost flower leaves with Mint Julep Green.

2. Using flat paintbrush, shade leaves with Arbor Green.

3. Using flat paintbrush, highlight leaves with Mint Julep Green + White.

4. Using scroller paintbrush, vein leaves with Arbor Green.

Flower Leaf Worksheet

1. Base-coat and shade.   2. Highlight. Vein.

Outer Flower Leaves & Small Tulip Leaves

1. Refer to Flower Leaf Worksheet on page 50 for outer flower leaves and Small Tulip Leaf Worksheet at right. Using flat paintbrush, base-coat outer flower leaves and all tulip leaves with Arbor Green.

2. Using flat paintbrush, shade outer flower leaves and all tulip leaves with Green Forest.

3. Using flat paintbrush, highlight outer flower leaves and all tulip leaves with Mint Julep Green.

4. Using scroller paintbrush, vein outer flower leaves and all tulip leaves with Green Forest.

Flowers

1. Refer to Flower Worksheet at right and on opposite page. Using flat paintbrush, base-coat flowers with Gooseberry Pink.

2. Using flat paintbrush, base-coat flower centers with Moon Yellow.

3. Using flat paintbrush, shade behind overlapping petals and behind flower centers with Antique Rose.

4. Using flat paintbrush, shade flower centers with Honey Brown.

Small Tulip Leaf Worksheet

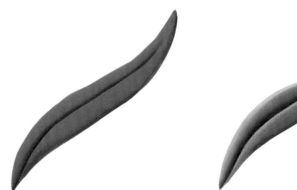

1. Base-coat and shade.   2. Highlight. Vein.

Flower Worksheet

1. Base-coat flower and center.   2. Shade flower and center.

3. Highlight flower and center.   4. Add linework.

Flower Worksheet

5. Dot center.

Small Tulip Worksheet

1. Base-coat.

2. Shade.

3. Highlight.

4. Highlight strokes.

5. Lay-down strokes.
Oval at base of tulip.

5. Using flat paintbrush, highlight flower petals with Gooseberry Pink + White.

6. Using liner paintbrush, line inside petals and crosshatch center with White.

7. Using end of paintbrush handle, paint varying dots around bottom of flower center with Red Iron Oxide.

Small Tulips
1. Refer to Small Tulip Worksheet at left. Using flat paintbrush, base-coat tulip petals with Antique Rose. Base-coat tulip centers with Gooseberry Pink.

2. Using flat paintbrush, shade inside area of tulip with Antique Rose.

3. Using flat paintbrush, shade petals with Red Iron Oxide.

4. Using flat paintbrush, highlight top center portion of tulip with Gooseberry Pink + White.

5. Using liner paintbrush, create highlight strokes on tulip with Gooseberry Pink + a little White.

6. Using liner paintbrush, paint lay-down strokes in center of tulip with White.

7. Using liner paintbrush, paint an oval at base of tulip with Red Iron Oxide.

Finish:
1. Apply several coats exterior satin spray varnish, following manufacturer's instructions.

Hydrangea Door

Materials

Painting Surface:
Prepainted door

Acrylic Paints:
D: Bungalow Blue
A: Celery Green
A: Charcoal
D: Grey Sky
D: Old Parchment

Paintbrushes:
Assorted flats
Mop
Old flat scruffy
Round
Soft-bristle: 3"

Supplies:
Disposable foam plates
  for varnish
Exterior water-based
  satin varnish
Liquid sander/
  deglosser
Palette
Palette knife
Paper towels
Retarder medium
Sandpaper
Stylus
Tack cloth
Water container
White transfer paper

I had a client who wanted a large hydrangea painted on her door. The door was painted taupe, so I chose colors for the flowers that would coordinate with the background color.

Instructions

Note: When making each wash, use one part paint to two parts water.

Surface Preparation:

1. Refer to Surface Preparation on pages 15–16.

2. Lightly sand the painting area for a better painting surface. Using tack cloth, wipe off any sawdust.

3. Using liquid sander/deglosser, wash over painting area.

4. Determine placement of motifs, then transfer Hydrangea Door Pattern on page 123 onto surface.

Paint:

1. Refer to Basic Painting Techniques on pages 11–15.

Hydrangeas

1. Refer to Hydrangea Worksheet on page 56. Using flat paintbrush, float all hydrangea petals with Grey Sky.

2. Mix a wash of Grey Sky. Using flat paintbrush, apply wash onto hydrangea petals.

3. Using flat paintbrush, paint hydrangea centers with Grey Sky + Charcoal.

4. Using flat paintbrush, shade behind all overlapping petals and where one hydrangea overlaps another with Grey Sky + Charcoal.

5. Using flat paintbrush, apply retarder medium onto one petal at a time. Using a round paintbrush, create a highlight stroke next to center at base of petal with Old Parchment. Using mop paintbrush, pull color up into petal. Soften by pouncing the paintbrush. Repeat for each petal.

Hydrangea Worksheet

1. Float petals.

2. Wash petals.

3. Paint center and shade overlapping petals.

4. Tint petals.

5. 2nd tint.

6. Add specks to center.

6. Using flat paintbrush, apply retarder medium onto one petal at a time. Using round paintbrush, create a second highlight stroke on base of petal with Celery Green. Using mop paintbrush, pull color up into petal. Do not cover all previously applied color. Blend colors by pouncing the paintbrush. Repeat for each petal.

7. Using old flat scruffy paintbrush, stipple around outside edge of hydrangea centers with Bungalow Blue. Note: Make certain to get a little blue around the edges of the hydrangea center.

Finish:

1. Using 3" soft-bristle paintbrush, apply three coats exterior water-based satin varnish, following manufacturer's instructions.

Angel Trumpet Potting Table

Materials

Painting Surface:
Sewing cabinet:
  29½" x 16½" x
  32" high

Acrylic Paints:
D: Autumn Brown
A: Buttermilk
A: Base Flesh
D: Dark Forest
  Green
D: Dunes Beige
D: Eucalyptus
A: Hot Shots
  Thermal Green
D: White

Paintbrushes:
Assorted flats
Chip: 2"
Mop

Supplies:
Cheesecloth
Decorative knobs
Disposable foam
  plates for varnish
Exterior satin
  paint: billiard
  green
Exterior water-
  based satin
  varnish
Foam paint roller
Hammer
Metal flashing
Old scissors
Palette
Palette knife
Paper towels
Plastic storage
  container to fit
  space for potting
  soil
Power sander and
  sand paper
Retarder medium
Routing tool
Ruler
Screwdriver
Scroll saw
Stain glaze: yellow
Stylus
Tack cloth
Translucent color
  glaze: buff; mocha
Water container
White transfer
  paper
Wire nails: #18 x ⅝"
Wood: 1" x 1" x 2'
Wood screws (4)

I got the idea for making this project from a crafting show on TV. I went to my local thrift store specifically to find a sewing cabinet and turn it into a potting table. After much consideration, I decided to paint it with Angel Trumpets.

Instructions

See photos on pages 2 and 57.

Surface Preparation:

1. Refer to Surface Preparation on pages 15–16.

2. Using screwdriver, remove all hardware from sewing cabinet. Remove sewing machine and all electrical works. Using power sander, sand rough areas for a better painting surface. Using tack cloth, wipe off any sawdust.

3. Using foam paint roller, base-coat entire sewing cabinet with billiard green exterior satin paint. Allow to dry and apply a second coat. Allow to dry 24 hours.

4. Using 2" chip paintbrush in a crisscross motion and overlapping strokes, apply a coat of buff color glaze onto sewing cabinet. Using a rolled up cheesecloth and pouncing up and down on surface, blend glaze to soften color and any brush strokes. Note: Work in small areas at a time so glaze does not dry before you can blend it out.

5. Repeat Step 4 with mocha color glaze. Allow to dry 24 hours.

6. Determine placement of motifs, then transfer Angel Trumpet Potting Table Patterns on pages 124–125 onto surface.

Paint:

1. Refer to Basic Painting Techniques on pages 11–15.

Angel Trumpets

1. Refer to Angel Trumpet Worksheet on opposite page. Using flat paintbrush, base-coat trumpets with Buttermilk.

2. Using flat paintbrush, apply retarder medium onto one trumpet at a time. Using flat paintbrush, shade trumpet with Dunes Beige. Soften, using a mop paintbrush. Repeat for each trumpet.

3. Using flat paintbrush, apply retarder medium onto one trumpet at a time. Using flat paintbrush, shade over previously shaded area with Base Flesh. Soften, using a mop paintbrush. Repeat for each trumpet. Note: The Base Flesh shading should not be mopped out as far.

4. Using flat paintbrush, apply retarder medium onto one trumpet at a time. Using flat paintbrush, shade darkest recesses of trumpet with Autumn Brown. Repeat for each trumpet.

5. Using flat paintbrush, apply retarder medium onto one trumpet at a time. Using flat paintbrush, highlight trumpets with White. Repeat for each trumpet.

6. Using flat paintbrush, apply retarder medium onto one trumpet at a time. Strengthen any shade or highlight as needed. Repeat for each trumpet.

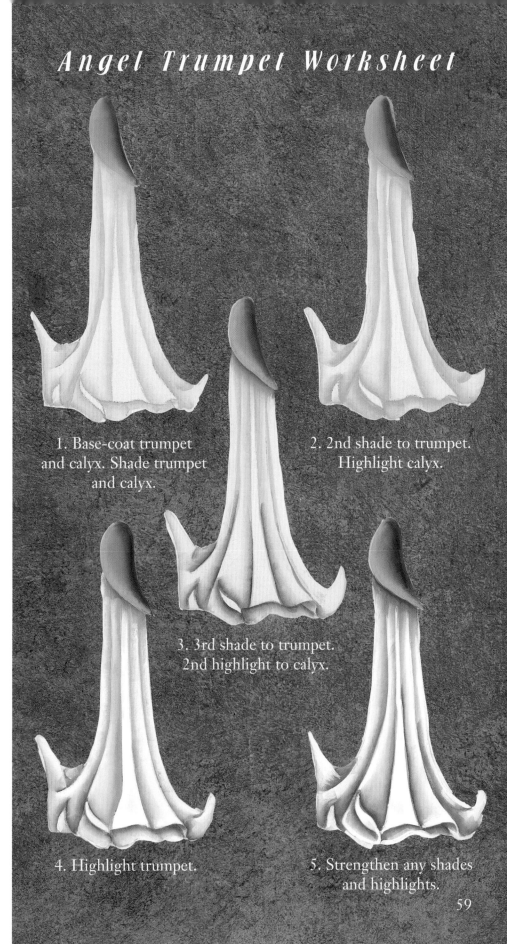

1. Base-coat trumpet and calyx. Shade trumpet and calyx.

2. 2nd shade to trumpet. Highlight calyx.

3. 3rd shade to trumpet. 2nd highlight to calyx.

4. Highlight trumpet.

5. Strengthen any shades and highlights.

Angel Trumpet Leaf Worksheet

1. Base-coat, shade, and vein.

2. Highlight.

3. Apply highlight to each section.

4. Highlight vein line and leaf side. Glaze.

5. Strengthen any shades. Tint.

Leaves

1. Refer to Angel Trumpet Leaf Worksheet above. Using flat paintbrush, base-coat leaves, calyx, and stems with Eucalyptus.

2. Using flat paintbrush, apply retarder medium onto one leaf at a time. Using flat paintbrush, shade leaf with Dark Forest Green. Soften, using a mop paintbrush. Repeat for each leaf.

3. Using flat paintbrush, apply retarder medium onto one leaf at a time. Using flat paintbrush, highlight top of leaf and vein with White + Eucalyptus. Soften, using a mop paintbrush. Repeat for each leaf.

4. Using flat paintbrush, stroke on highlight color between each vein line from highlight side of vein to bottom of leaf.

5. Using flat paintbrush, stroke on highlight color on shade side of vein from bottom of leaf up toward vein. Note: Take care to avoid going into the shaded area.

6. Using flat paintbrush, apply retarder medium onto one leaf at a time. Using flat paintbrush, highlight vein area and edge of leaf with Hot Shots Thermal Green. Repeat for each leaf.

7. Mix one part yellow stain glaze to one part water. Using flat paintbrush, apply wash over leaves.

8. Using flat paintbrush, apply retarder medium onto one leaf at a time. Strengthen any shade, vein, or highlight as needed. Repeat for each leaf.

9. Using flat paintbrush, apply retarder medium onto one leaf at a time. Using flat paintbrush, randomly tint leaf with Base Flesh. Soften, using a mop paintbrush. Repeat for each leaf.

10. Using flat paintbrush, apply retarder medium onto one stem or calyx at a time. Using flat paintbrush, shade stem or calyx with Dark Forest Green. Repeat for each.

11. Using flat paintbrush, apply retarder medium onto one stem or calyx at a time. Using flat paintbrush, highlight stem or calyx with White + Eucalyptus. Repeat for each.

12. Using flat paintbrush, apply retarder medium onto one stem or calyx at a time. Using flat paintbrush, apply a float over previously highlighted area with Hot Shots Thermal Green. Repeat for each.

Finish:

1. Apply three coats exterior water-based satin varnish, following manufacturer's instructions.

Assembly:

1. Cover lid and inside top surface of sewing cabinet with metal flashing to protect work surface.

2. Set individual sewing cabinet pieces on flashing. Using a stylus, trace around pieces to score the flashing.

3. Using an old pair of scissors, cut out flashing.

4. Hammer flashing onto each piece of sewing cabinet where needed.

5. To do top portion of sewing cabinet, measure flashing to fit. Cut out where opening is that sewing machine occupied. Hammer into place.

6. Using scroll saw, cut one 9" piece and one 12" piece from 1" x 1" board. Using routing tool, cut a ⅜" x ½" rabbet in one side of each piece. Using screwdriver, attach each piece within the opening with two wood screws to hold a plastic storage container for potting soil in place.

7. Using screwdriver, reassemble sewing cabinet with hinges and screws.

8. Attach decorative knobs onto drawers.

Tulip Pedestal

I purchased this plain metal pedestal with the idea that it would be perfect for showing off flowers from my cutting garden. The large tulip fit it just right.

Materials

Painting Surface:
Metal pedestal: 10" square
x 36" high

Acrylic Paints:
D: Black
D: Dark Foliage
D: Dusty Purple
D: Medium Foliage
A: Pink Chiffon
D: Royal Plum
D: Village Green
D: Wisteria
D: White

Paintbrushes:
Assorted flats
Mop

Supplies:
Black transfer paper
Exterior satin paint: white
Exterior spray primer
Exterior satin spray
  varnish
Foam paint roller
Palette
Palette knife
Paper towels
Retarder medium
Sandpaper
Stylus
Tack cloth
Towel
Water container
Wool pad applicator

Instructions

Note: When making each wash, use one part paint to two parts water.

Surface Preparation:

1. Refer to Surface Preparation on pages 15–16.

2. Lightly sand to roughen surface. Using tack cloth, wipe off any dust.

3. Apply several coats exterior spray primer, following manufacturer's instructions. Allow to dry 24 hours.

4. Mix white exterior paint + a little Black to grey it slightly. Mix in a little Wisteria to yield a Light Lavender mixture.

5. Using foam paint roller, paint pedestal until it is opaque with Light Lavender mixture.

6. Mix a wash of Light Lavender mixture, a wash of Light Lavender mixture + Wisteria, and a wash of White.

7. Dampen wool pad applicator with water. Blot excess water onto a towel until applicator is only slightly damp. Randomly brush each color wash directly onto applicator.

8. Randomly apply color washes onto one side of pedestal, pouncing applicator up and down over surface to soften and mottle colors. Note: If more color is needed in an area, reapply color washes where needed. Soften, using applicator. Allow to dry.

9. Repeat Steps 7–8 on remaining sides and top. Allow to dry.

10. Determine placement of motif, then transfer Tulip Pedestal Pattern on page 126 onto surface. Note: Keep transfer light as you will be painting with washes of color.

Large Tulip Worksheet

1. Float and wash.

2. Shade.

3. 2nd shade.

4. 3rd shade.

5. Highlight. Strengthen shades as needed.

Paint:
1. Refer to Basic Painting Techniques on pages 11–15.

Large Tulip
1. Refer to Large Tulip Worksheet at left. Using flat paintbrush, float all lines on tulip with Wisteria.

2. Mix a wash of Wisteria. Using flat paintbrush, apply wash onto tulip.

3. Using flat paintbrush, apply retarder medium onto tulip. Using flat paintbrush, shade tulip with Wisteria. Soften, using a mop paintbrush.

4. Using flat paintbrush, apply retarder medium onto tulip. Using flat paintbrush, shade tulip with Dusty Purple, taking care to avoid covering all the previously floated color. Soften, using a mop paintbrush.

5. Using flat paintbrush, apply retarder medium onto tulip. Using flat paintbrush, shade tulip with Royal Plum. Soften, using a mop paintbrush. Repeat as needed. Note: Do not float every previously shaded area with Royal Plum. It should be randomly applied to areas that need to be darkened.

6. Using flat paintbrush, apply retarder medium onto tulip. Using flat paintbrush, highlight tulip with Pink Chiffon. Soften, using a mop paintbrush.

7. Using flat paintbrush, apply retarder medium onto tulip. Using flat paintbrush, highlight tulip with White + Wisteria. Soften, using a mop paintbrush.

Large Tulip Leaves
1. Refer to Large Tulip Leaf Worksheet at right and on page 66. Using flat paintbrush, float all lines on leaves with Village Green.

2. Mix a wash of Village Green. Using flat paintbrush, apply wash onto leaves.

3. Using flat paintbrush, apply retarder medium onto one leaf at a time. Using flat paintbrush, shade leaf with Medium Foliage. Soften, using a mop paintbrush. Repeat for each leaf.

4. Using flat paintbrush, apply retarder medium onto one leaf at a time. Using flat paintbrush, shade leaf with Dark Foliage, taking care to avoid covering all the previously floated color. Soften, using a mop paintbrush. Repeat for each leaf.

5. Using flat paintbrush, apply retarder medium onto one leaf at a time. Using flat paintbrush, shade leaf with Dark Foliage + Black. Soften, using a mop paintbrush. Repeat as needed. Note: Do not float every previously shaded area with Dark Foliage + Black. It should be randomly applied to areas that need to be darkened.

6. Using flat paintbrush, apply retarder medium onto one leaf at a time. Using flat paintbrush, highlight leaf with Village Green. Soften, using a mop paintbrush. Repeat for each leaf.

Finish:
1. Apply three coats exterior satin spray varnish, following manufacturer's instructions.

Large Tulip Leaf Worksheet

1. Float and wash.

2. Shade.

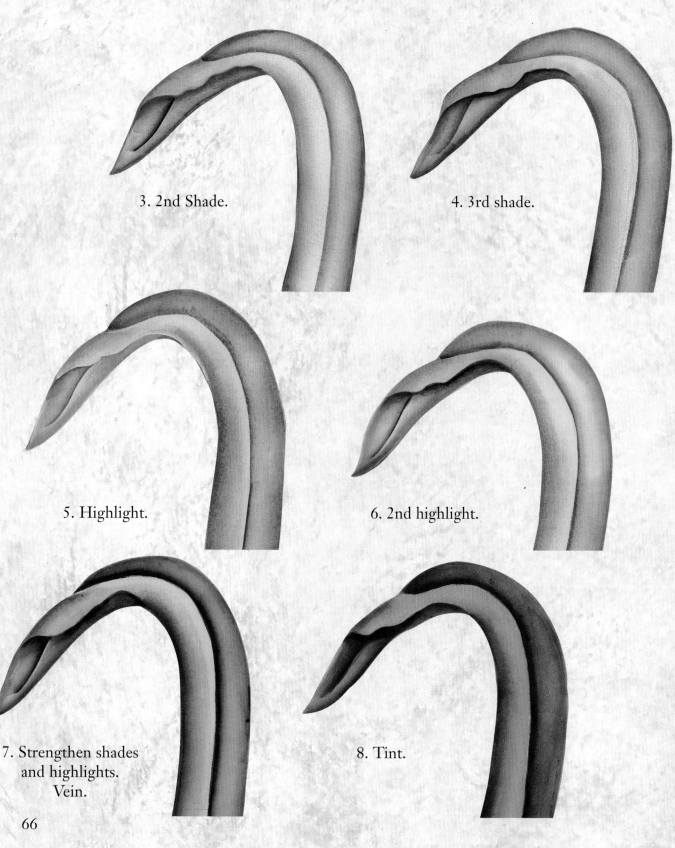

3. 2nd Shade.

4. 3rd shade.

5. Highlight.

6. 2nd highlight.

7. Strengthen shades
   and highlights.
   Vein.

8. Tint.

Second-hand Chic Table

Second-hand Chic Table

Materials

Painting Surface:
Wooden table: 44" dia.

Acrylic Paints:
D: Bahama Purple
A: Black Green
D: Bridgeport Grey
F: Burnt Carmine
D: Burnt Sienna
A: Deep Midnight Blue
A: Driftwood
A: Dusty Sage
D: Eucalyptus
A: Evergreen
A: Honey Brown
A: Light Buttermilk
A: Moon Yellow
D: Red Iron Oxide
D: Rhythm 'N Blue
D: Rosetta Pink
A: Silver Sage Green
A: Soft blue
D: White

Paintbrushes:
Assorted flats
Liner
Mop
Old flat scruffy
Round
Scroller

Supplies:
Black transfer paper
Clean soft rag
Disposable foam plates
 for varnish
Exterior satin paint:
 off-white
Exterior water-based
 satin varnish
Foam paint roller
Palette
Palette knife
Paper towels
Power sander and
 sandpapers: 60-grit;
 220-grit
Retarder medium
Stylus
Tack cloth
Water container

I found this round table at a local thrift store for $30. It struck me that this would make a great piece for a floral design. I couldn't wait to get started making this old brown table into something beautiful.

Instructions

See photo on page 67.

Note: Unless otherwise directed, use one part paint to two parts water when making each wash.

Surface Preparation:
1. Refer to Surface Preparation on pages 15–16.

2. Using power sander and 60-grit sandpaper, lightly sand for a better painting surface. Using tack cloth, wipe off any dust.

3. Using foam paint roller, paint table with off-white exterior paint. Allow to dry 24 hours.

4. Using power sander and 220-grit sandpaper, lightly sand the painted table. Using tack cloth, wipe off any dust. Apply a second coat of off-white exterior paint.

5. Mix a wash of Driftwood. Using foam paint roller, apply wash onto table. Using a clean soft rag, lightly wipe off wash so it streaks, creating a weathered look. Repeat for base and legs of table. Allow to dry overnight.

6. Determine placement of motifs, then transfer Second-hand Chic Table Patterns on pages 127–132 onto surface. Note: Keep transfer light as you will be painting with washes of color.

Paint:
1. Refer to Basic Painting Techniques on pages 11–15.

Blossom Leaves

1. Refer to Blossom Leaf Worksheet at right.

2. Mix a wash of Eucalyptus. Using flat paintbrush, apply wash onto all leaves.

3. Using flat paintbrush, apply retarder medium onto one leaf at a time. Using flat paintbrush, shade leaf with Dusty Sage. Repeat for each leaf.

4. Using flat paintbrush, apply retarder medium onto one leaf at a time. Using flat paintbrush, shade over previous shading with Evergreen. Repeat for each leaf.

5. Using flat paintbrush, apply retarder medium onto one leaf at a time. Using flat paintbrush, highlight leaf with Silver Sage Green. Repeat for each leaf.

6. Using scroller paintbrush, paint stems, tendrils, and veins on all leaves with Evergreen.

Blossoms

1. Refer to Blossom Worksheet at right and on page 70.

2. Mix a wash of Bridgeport Grey. Using flat paintbrush, apply wash onto all blossoms.

3. Using flat paintbrush, apply retarder medium onto one blossom at a time. Using flat paintbrush, shade behind blossom center and behind overlapping petals with Bahama Purple. Repeat for each blossom.

4. Using flat paintbrush, apply retarder medium onto one blossom at a time. Using flat paintbrush, shade over previous blossom shading with Rhythm 'N Blue. Repeat for each blossom.

5. Using flat paintbrush, apply retarder medium onto one blossom at a time. Using flat paintbrush,

Blossom Leaf Worksheet

1. Wash and shade.   2. 2nd shade.

3. Highlight.   4. Tint and add vein.

Blossom Worksheet

1. Wash and shade.   2. 2nd shade.

3. 3rd shade. Highlight.   4. Wash center.

highlight petals with Soft Blue. Repeat for each blossom. Note: If needed, add a little White to Soft Blue.

6. Mix a wash of Moon Yellow. Using flat paintbrush, apply wash onto all blossom centers.

7. Using old flat scruffy paintbrush, create a highlight by stippling over top portion of blossom center with Light Buttermilk.

8. Using flat paintbrush, shade bottom of blossom center with Burnt Sienna. Repeat for each blossom.

9. Mix a wash of Honey Brown. Using flat paintbrush, apply wash onto all blossom centers.

10. Using liner paintbrush, dab around each blossom center with Deep Midnight Blue.

Large Roses
1. Refer to Large Rose Worksheet at right and on opposite page.

2. Mix a wash of Rosetta Pink. Using flat paintbrush, apply wash onto large roses.

3. Using flat paintbrush, apply retarder medium onto one rose at a time. Using flat paintbrush, shade rose with Red Iron Oxide. Repeat for each rose.

4. Using flat paintbrush, apply retarder medium onto one rose at a time. Using flat paintbrush, shade over previous rose shading with Red Iron Oxide + Burnt Carmine. Repeat for each rose.

5. Using flat paintbrush, apply retarder medium onto one rose at a time. Using flat paintbrush, highlight rose with Rosetta Pink + Light Buttermilk. Repeat for each rose.

6. Using liner paintbrush, dab rose centers with Moon Yellow.

Blossom Worksheet

5. Stipple highlight on center.

6. Wash center. Shade center.

7. Dab center.

Large Rose Worksheet

1. Wash and shade.

2. Shade behind first row of petals in throat.

Large Rose Worksheet

3. Shade behind remaining rows of petals in throat.

4. 2nd shade. Highlight.

5. Dab throat.

Small Rose & Bud Worksheet

1. Wash and shade.

2. 2nd shade. Highlight.

3. Dab throat.

Small Roses & Buds

1. Refer to Small Rose & Bud Worksheet above.

2. Mix a wash of Red Iron Oxide. Using flat paintbrush, apply wash onto small roses and buds.

3. Using flat paintbrush, apply retarder medium onto one rose or bud at a time. Using flat paintbrush, shade rose or bud with Red Iron Oxide. Repeat for each rose or bud.

4. Using flat paintbrush, apply retarder medium onto one rose or bud at a time. Using flat paintbrush, shade over previous rose or bud shading with Burnt Carmine. Repeat for each rose or bud.

5. Using flat paintbrush, apply retarder medium onto one rose or bud at a time. Using flat paintbrush, highlight rose or bud with Rosetta Pink. Repeat for each rose or bud.

6. Using liner paintbrush, dab rose centers with Moon Yellow.

7. Using round paintbrush, paint calyx on buds, following instructions for Blossom Leaves on page 69.

Daisy Worksheet

1. Base-coat and shade.

2. Highlight petals.
Base-coat center.

3. Stipple highlight
on center.

4. Shade center. Tint petals.

5. Dot center.

Daisies

1. Refer to Daisy Worksheet above.

2. Mix a wash of Light Buttermilk. Using round paintbrush, apply wash onto daisies.

3. Using flat paintbrush, apply retarder medium onto one daisy at a time. Using flat paintbrush, highlight each petal with Light Buttermilk. Repeat for each daisy.

4. Using flat paintbrush, apply retarder medium onto one daisy at a time. Using flat paintbrush, shade behind overlapping petal and behind daisy center with Bridgeport Grey. Soften, using mop paintbrush. Repeat for each daisy.

5. Using flat paintbrush, tint petals with any of the following colors: Bahama Purple, Moon Yellow, Rhythm 'N Blue, Red Iron Oxide, or Rosetta Pink. Soften, using mop paintbrush. Note: Tint daisy petals with the color of the closest flower.

6. Mix a wash of Moon Yellow. Using flat paintbrush, apply wash onto daisy centers.

7. Using old flat scruffy paintbrush, create a highlight by stippling with Light Buttermilk.

8. Using flat paintbrush, apply retarder medium onto one daisy center at a time. Using flat

paintbrush, shade bottom of daisy center and inside C-shaped strokes with Burnt Sienna. Repeat for each daisy center.

9. Using end of paintbrush handle, paint various sized dots around daisy centers with Black Green.

Finish:

1. At this point, colors will be very vivid and will not look like the sample shown here. If this look is desired, apply three coats of exterior water-based satin varnish, following manufacturer's instructions.

2. For the faded appearance shown, mix a wash of one part White to three parts water.

3. Using foam paint roller and working quickly, apply wash onto table. Note: If bubbles appear, roll over them and they will disappear as the wash begins to dry. Allow to dry overnight. Apply the wash repeatedly until desired look is achieved. Make certain to let each coat dry before applying another.

4. Using foam paint roller, apply three coats of exterior satin varnish, following manufacturer's instructions.

Autumn Leaves Hutch

Materials

Painting Surface:
Wooden hutch:
  23" x 16" x 33" high

Acrylic Paints:
D: Autumn Brown
D: Black
A: Black Forest Green
D: Burnt Sienna
D: Chocolate Cherry
A: Dark Chocolate
A: Forest Green
A: Honey Brown
A: Jade Green
L: Light Lime
A: Moon Yellow
A: Napa Red
A: Red Iron Oxide
L: True Orange
L: True Poppy
L: True Red
D: White

Paintbrushes:
Assorted flats
Mop
Round
Scroller
Soft-bristle: 3"

Supplies:
Ballpoint pen
Chalk
Disposable foam plates
  for varnish
Exterior water-based
  matte varnish
Packaging tape, clear
Palette
Palette knife
Paper towels
Retarder medium
Stylus
Water container

I found this cabinet/hutch at a local craft boutique. I loved it for its rustic charm and I knew that just a bit of paint would make it special.

Instructions

Note: The rough wood on this particular piece makes the process of transferring the pattern very difficult. To make it stronger, cover the entire traced pattern with clear packaging tape. Chalk the back of the pattern. After arranging the pattern on the piece as desired, trace around it, using a ballpoint pen and applying a good amount of pressure.

Surface Preparation:
1. Refer to Surface Preparation on pages 15–16.

2. Determine placement of motifs, then transfer Autumn Leaves Hutch Patterns on page 132 onto surface. Using chalk, mark placement of branch.

Paint:
1. Refer to Basic Painting Techniques on pages 11–15.

Leaves
1. Refer to Autumn Leaf Worksheet and Leaf Legend on page 76. Using flat paintbrush, base-coat each leaf with color indicated.

2. Using flat paintbrush, apply retarder medium onto one leaf at a time. Using flat paintbrush, shade leaf with color(s) indicated. Soften, using mop paintbrush. Repeat for each leaf.

3. Using flat paintbrush, apply retarder medium onto one leaf at a time. Using flat paintbrush, highlight leaf with color(s) indicated. Soften, using mop paintbrush. Repeat for each leaf.

4. Using scroller paintbrush, vein all leaves with Dark Chocolate. Add a little Black to Dark Chocolate where dimension is needed.

Autumn Leaf Worksheet

Leaf Legend

Red Leaves:
Base-coat: True Red
Shade: Chocolate Cherry
Highlight: True Poppy

Orange Leaves:
Base-coat: Red Iron Oxide
Shade: Napa Red
Highlight: True Orange

Gold Leaves:
Base-coat: Honey Brown
Shade: Burnt Sienna
Highlight: Moon Yellow
2nd Highlight: Light Lime

Yellow Leaves:
Base-coat: Moon Yellow
Shade: Honey Brown
2nd Shade: Burnt Sienna
Highlight: True Orange or
    True Poppy

Green Leaves:
Base-coat: Jade Green
Shade: Forest Green
2nd Shade: Black Forest Green
Highlight: Light Lime

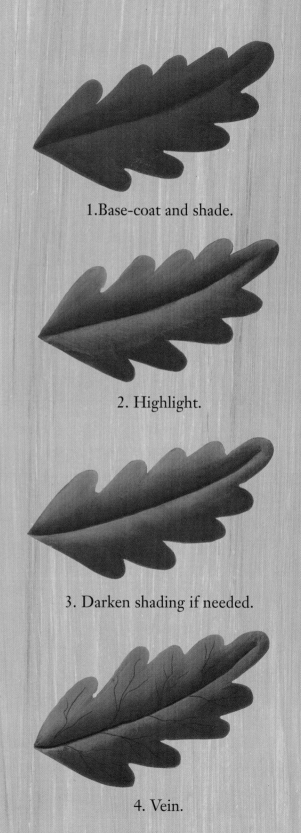

1. Base-coat and shade.

2. Highlight.

3. Darken shading if needed.

4. Vein.

Acorns

1. Refer to Acorn Worksheet at right. Using flat paintbrush, base-coat each acorn with Autumn Brown + White.

2. Using flat paintbrush, shade acorns with Autumn Brown.

3. Using flat paintbrush, highlight acorns with White + Autumn Brown.

4. Using flat paintbrush, create a highlight stroke on each acorn with White.

5. Using flat paintbrush, base-coat each acorn cap with Autumn Brown.

6. Using flat paintbrush, shade each acorn cap with Dark Chocolate.

7. Using flat paintbrush, highlight each acorn cap with Autumn Brown + White.

8. Using scroller paintbrush, line each acorn cap with Dark Chocolate + Black.

Branch

1. Refer to Branch Worksheet at right. Using round paintbrush, paint branch with Autumn Brown.

2. Using flat paintbrush, shade branch with Dark Chocolate.

3. Using flat paintbrush, highlight branch with Autumn Brown + White.

Finish:

1. Using 3" soft-bristle paintbrush, apply three coats exterior water-based matte varnish, following manufacturer's instructions.

Acorn Worksheet

1. Base-coat and shade.   2. Highlight.   3. Add lines.

Branch Worksheet

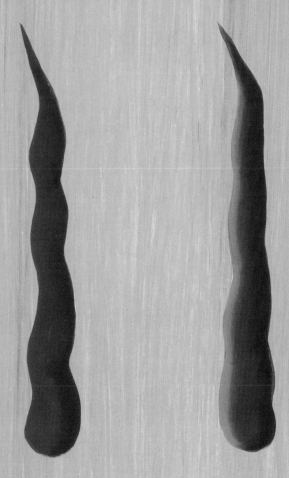

1. Base-coat and shade.   2. Highlight.

Materials

Painting Surfaces:
Stop molding: 1⅛" x
    length of shelf
Twig shelves

Acrylic Paints:
D: Black
D: Burnt Umber
D: Cinnamon
D: Dark Brown
A: Driftwood
A: Hot Shots Fiery Red
D: Lichen Grey
A: Light Buttermilk
A: Sable Brown
D: Tuscan Red

Paintbrushes:
Assorted flats
Flogger
Liner
Scroller

Supplies:
Disposable foam plates
    for varnish
Exterior water-based
    satin varnish
Finishing nails: 1"
Hammer
Palette
Palette knife
Paper towels
Water container
Wood glue

When I saw this twig shelving unit at a local thrift store for only $10, I knew I had to have it! Initially, I couldn't decide where to paint on it, as I intended to fill the shelves with flowers and my favorite garden items. Finally, I decided to add molding to the front of each shelf and paint that.

Instructions

Note: When making each wash, use one part paint to two parts water.

Surface Preparation:

1. Refer to Surface Preparation on pages 15–16.

2. Using flat paintbrush, paint molding with a wash of Lichen Grey.

3. Using flat paintbrush, dry-brush here and there with Driftwood.

4. Using flogger paintbrush, dry-brush length of molding with Sable Brown to add wood-grain look.

Paint:

1. Refer to Basic Painting Techniques on pages 11–15.

Vines

1. Refer to Vines, Leaves & Berries Worksheet on page 80. Using scroller paintbrush and making varied thin and thick strokes, paint vines along length of each piece of molding with Dark Brown.

2. Using scroller paintbrush and making thin and thick strokes, add more vines with Burnt Umber.

Leaves

1. Refer to Vines, Leaves & Berries Worksheet on page 80. Mix a wash of Dark Brown and a wash of Burnt Umber. Using flat paintbrush, stroke leaves on vines with each wash.

2. Using scroller paintbrush, add stems and veins on all leaves with Burnt Umber.

(continued on page 81)

Vines, Leaves & Berries Worksheet

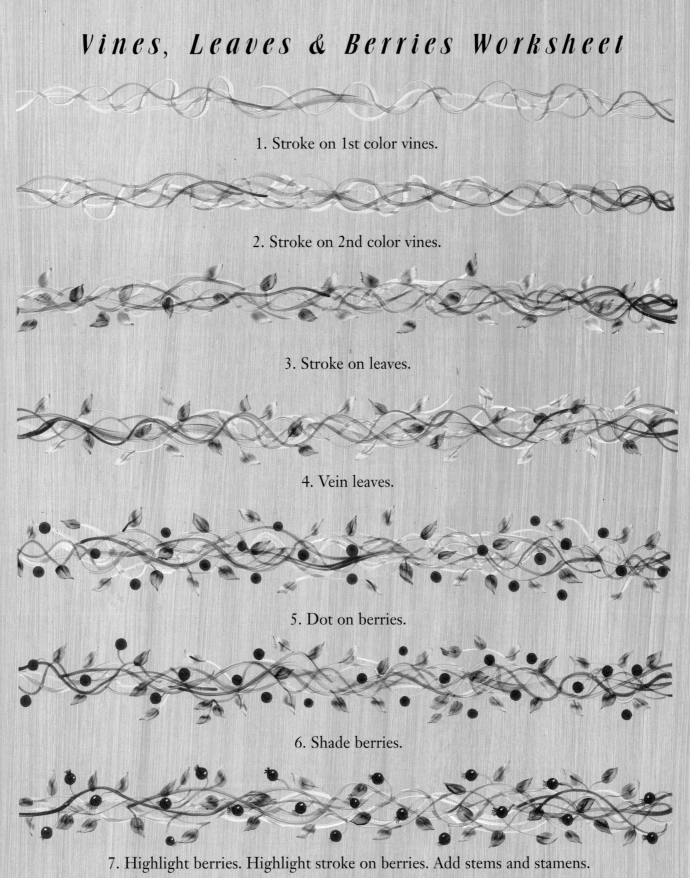

1. Stroke on 1st color vines.

2. Stroke on 2nd color vines.

3. Stroke on leaves.

4. Vein leaves.

5. Dot on berries.

6. Shade berries.

7. Highlight berries. Highlight stroke on berries. Add stems and stamens.

(continued from page 78)

Berries

1. Refer to Vines, Leaves & Berries Worksheet on opposite page. Using end of paintbrush handle, paint a large dot for each berry on vines with Tuscan Red.

2. Using flat paintbrush, shade bottom or left side of each berry with Cinnamon.

3. Using flat paintbrush, highlight each berry on the top or right side with Hot Shots Fiery Red.

4. Using liner paintbrush, add a small highlight stroke with Light Buttermilk.

5. Using liner paintbrush, paint berry stems and stamens with Burnt Umber + a little Black.

Finish:

1. Apply several coats exterior water-based satin varnish, following manufacturer's instructions.

Assembly:

1. Apply beads of wood glue along the edge of the shelf. Press molding onto shelf and hammer in place with finishing nails. Hint: Using a second finishing nail, place the point on top of the original finishing nail. Tap the nail slightly to sink original nail below the molding's surface.

Gaillardia & Dahlia Washtubs

Materials

Painting Surfaces:
Metal washtubs and
    stand: 20½" square x
    32" high (in stand)

Acrylic Paints:
D: Black
D: Cinnamon
D: Crocus Yellow
D: Dark Foliage
A: Hot Shots Fiery Red
A: Hot Shots Scorching
    Yellow
A: Light Buttermilk
D: Light Foliage
A: Marigold
D: Medium Foliage
A: Napa Red
D: Poppy Orange
D: Pumpkin
D: Tuscan Red
D: White

Paintbrushes:
Assorted flats
Assorted rounds
Liner
Mop
Old flat scruffy
Scroller

Supplies:
Exterior satin spray paint:
    black
Exterior satin spray
    varnish
Exterior spray primer
Palette
Palette knife
Paper towels
Retarder medium
Sandpaper
Stylus
Tack cloth
Water container
White transfer paper

You can plant your favorite flowers in these old-time metal washtubs or fill them with ice and soft drinks for a summer garden party.

Instructions

Surface Preparation:

1. Refer to Surface Preparation on pages 15–16.

2. Lightly sand the painting area to remove any rust from painting surface. Using tack cloth, wipe off any dust.

3. Apply several coats exterior spray primer to surface, following manufacturer's instructions. Allow to dry 24 hours.

4. Apply several coats black exterior spray paint, following manufacturer's instructions. Allow to dry 24 hours.

5. Determine placement of motifs, then transfer Gaillardia & Dahlia Washtubs Pattern on page 133 onto surface.

Paint:

1. Refer to Basic Painting Techniques on pages 11–15.

Gaillardias & Buds

1. Refer to Gaillardia & Bud Worksheets on pages 84–86. Using flat paintbrush, base-coat flowers and buds on washtubs with Marigold until opaque.

2. Using flat paintbrush, apply retarder medium onto one gaillardia or bud at a time. Using flat paintbrush, shade behind overlapping petals with Tuscan Red. Shade petals behind gaillardia center with a wide float of Tuscan Red. Repeat for each gaillardia or bud.

3. Using flat paintbrush, shade over previous float with Cinnamon. Note: This shade should not be as wide as the previous float and should be used only in the darkest areas.

4. Using flat paintbrush, highlight overlapping petals with Crocus Yellow.

(continued on page 86)

1. Base-coat flower.

2. Shade flower petals.

3. Shade behind center.

4. Apply 2nd shade color to petals and behind center.

5. Highlight petals.

6. 2nd highlight.

7. Line petals.

8. Stipple shade on center.

9. Stipple 2nd shade on center.

10. Dot center.

Gaillardia & Bud Worksheet

11. Add lay-down strokes.

1. Base-coat and shade.

2. 2nd shade.

3. Highlight petals.

4. Stipple on center.

5. Dot center. Highlight calyx.

(continued from page 82)

5. Using flat paintbrush, highlight over previous highlights on petals with Hot Shots Scorching Yellow.

6. Using scroller paintbrush, line all gaillardia petals with Tuscan Red + Cinnamon. Note: Do not line petals of buds.

7. Using old flat scruffy paintbrush, stipple gaillardia centers and buds with Crocus Yellow.

8. Using old flat scruffy paintbrush, stipple over gaillardia centers with Tuscan Red, leaving a little highlight of Crocus Yellow in the center.

9. Using old flat scruffy paintbrush, stipple over gaillardia centers with Cinnamon, leaving the Tuscan Red and Crocus Yellow colors still showing through.

10. Using end of paintbrush handle, paint various sized dots onto gaillardia centers and buds with Cinnamon.

11. Using liner paintbrush, paint lay-down stokes around outside of gaillardia centers with Crocus Yellow. Note: Do not paint lay-down strokes around buds.

12. Using round paintbrush, paint calyx with Medium Foliage.

13. Using flat paintbrush, highlight calyx with Light Foliage.

14. Using round paintbrush, paint stems with Medium Foliage.

Dahlias & Buds

1. Refer to Dahlia Worksheet on opposite page. Using flat paintbrush, base-coat dahlias and buds with Light Buttermilk.

2. Using small round paintbrush and working from the center outward, paint strokes of various lengths on each dahlia petal and bud with Napa Red.

3. Using liner paintbrush and pulling from the bottom up on each bud petal, paint strokes with Napa Red.

4. Using flat paintbrush, shade behind overlapping petals and dahlia centers with Napa Red + a little Black.

5. Using flat paintbrush, highlight overlapping petals over previously shaded areas with Hot Shots Fiery Red.

6. Using flat paintbrush, highlight tips of petals with White.

7. Using small round paintbrush, paint calyx on buds with Medium Foliage.

8. Using flat paintbrush, highlight calyx on buds with Light Foliage.

9. Using old flat scruffy paintbrush, stipple dahlia centers with Poppy Orange until opaque.

10. Using liner paintbrush and working from the outside inward, paint lay-down strokes on dahlia centers with Pumpkin until most of the center is filled in.

#1 Leaves

1. Refer to #1 Leaf Worksheet on page 88. Using flat paintbrush, base-coat #1 leaves with Light Foliage.

2. Using flat paintbrush, shade leaves with Medium Foliage.

3. Using flat paintbrush, highlight leaves with Light Foliage + White.

Dahlia Worksheet

1. Base-coat flower and center.

2. Paint strokes on each petal.

3. Shade petals and behind center.

4. Highlight red portion of petals.

5. Highlight tips of petals.

6. Stipple center. Apply lay-down strokes.

4. Using flat paintbrush, apply retarder medium onto one leaf at a time. Using flat paintbrush, tint leaf with any of the following colors: Napa Red, Cinnamon, Crocus Yellow, Tuscan Red, Poppy Orange, or Pumpkin. Soften, using mop paintbrush. Repeat for each leaf.

5. Using scroller paintbrush, vein leaves with Dark Foliage.

#1 Leaf Worksheet

1. Base-coat. 2. Shade.

3. Highlight. 4. Tint.

#2 Leaf Worksheet

1. Base-coat. 2. Shade.

3. Highlight. 4. Tint.

#2 Leaves

1. Refer to #2 Leaf Worksheet at left. Using flat paintbrush, base-coat #2 leaves with Medium Foliage.

2. Using flat paintbrush, shade leaves with Dark Foliage.

3. Using flat paintbrush, highlight leaves with Light Foliage.

4. Using flat paintbrush, apply retarder medium onto one leaf at a time. Using flat paintbrush, tint leaf with any of the following colors: Cinnamon, Crocus Yellow, Napa Red, Poppy Orange, Pumpkin, or Tuscan Red. Soften, using mop paintbrush. Repeat for each leaf.

5. Using scroller paintbrush, vein leaves with Dark Foliage. If needed, add a little Black to the Dark Foliage.

6. Using scroller paintbrush, paint tendrils with Medium Foliage.

Vine

1. Using scroller paintbrush, stroke on vine with Medium Foliage.

2. Using flat paintbrush, stroke on leaves with a double load of Light Foliage and Dark Foliage.

Stand

1. Vine on the stand is completed as instructed above. Dahlias and larger leaves are painted as instructed above.

2. Outline the curves of the legs with Medium Foliage.

Finish:

1. Apply several coats exterior satin spray varnish, following manufacturer's instructions.

88

Romantic Roses Bench

Materials

Painting Surface:
Old headboard and
  footboard: twin size
Birch plywood for seat:
  12½" x 36" x 1" thick

Acrylic Paints:
F: Butterscotch
F: Down Home Brown
  Antique Medium
D: Eucalyptus
A: Marigold
D: Old Parchment
D: White

Paintbrushes:
Angular: ½"
Assorted flats
Chip: 2"
Liner
Mop
Scroller
Soft-bristle stencil

Supplies:
Black transfer paper
Clean soft rags
Craft knife or electric stencil
  cutter
Disposable foam bowls for
  mixing paint
Disposable foam plates
  for varnish
Exterior satin paint: pure
  white (½ gallon)
Exterior water-based satin
  varnish
Foam paint roller
Mylar®: 5mm
Palette
Palette knife
Paper towels
Power drill and drill bits
Power sander and sandpaper
Retarder medium
Screwdriver
Scroll saw
Stencil adhesive
Stylus
Tack cloth
Water container
Water-based glaze medium
Wood: 2" x 4" x 8'
Wood filler
Wood screws: 3½" (24)

I had an old twin sized headboard and footboard made into a bench and painted a rose in full bloom on it that is so life-like it fools the bees.

Instructions

See photos on pages 6–7 and 89.

Surface Preparation:

1. Refer to Surface Preparation on pages 15–16.

2. Using power sander, sand surface to prepare it to be painted. Using tack cloth, wipe off any sawdust.

3. Using large flat paintbrush and foam paint roller, base-coat seat, headboard, and footboard with pure white exterior satin paint. Repeat for two coats.

4. Transfer Romantic Roses Stencil Pattern on page 135 onto Mylar with black transfer paper. Using craft knife or electric stencil cutter, cut pattern from Mylar to create a stencil.

5. In disposable bowl, mix one part Old Parchment to two parts glaze medium.

6. Determine placement of motifs, then adhere stencil onto surface.

7. Using soft-bristle stencil paintbrush, stencil design onto headboard and footboard with Old Parchment mixture.

8. Repeat Steps 6–7 as needed to complete headboard and footboard.

9. Using chip paintbrush, randomly apply Down Home Brown Antique Medium over surface. Wipe off, using a clean soft rag.

10. Determine placement of motifs, then transfer Romantic Roses Bench Pattern on page 134 onto surface.

Paint:

1. Refer to Basic Painting Techniques on pages 11–15.

Rose

1. Refer to Rose Worksheet below and on page 92. Using flat paintbrush, base-coat rose shape with Marigold.

2. Using flat paintbrush, shade inside and bottom of bowl and petals next to bowl with Butterscotch.

3. Using double-loaded flat paintbrush, stroke on top row of petals with Marigold and White—with White edge of paintbrush toward top of rose. Immediately stroke on another row slightly below the first. Continue for approximately five rows of petals.

4. Using double-loaded flat paintbrush, stroke to connect left and right sides inside bowl with Marigold and White—with White edge of paintbrush toward top of rose. Double-load paintbrush again and apply 2nd, 3rd, 4th, and 5th stroke to complete the rose bowl. Each section of the rose should be slightly lower than the previous one. Note: It is important begin this stroke with a chisel edge, pull it to a flat edge, and return to a chisel edge to finish the stroke. The stroke should be U-shaped to create depth.

5. Using double-loaded flat paintbrush, stroke on the side petals with Marigold and White—keeping the White edge of paintbrush toward outside of petals. Note: First, do the top left and right petals. Then do bottom petals and complete the flower with the center petal, chiseling the brush off and tucking the stroke under one of the bottom petals to avoid a blunt, squared-off edge.

6. Using flat paintbrush, shade inside bowl, bottom of bowl, and base of each petal with Butterscotch.

7. Using flat paintbrush, float behind each row with Butterscotch for more distinction between rows of petals on the bowl. Note: This step is optional.

(continued on page 93)

Rose Worksheet

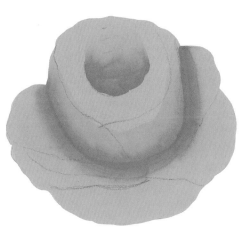

1. Base-coat and shade.

2. Stroke on back petals of bowl.

Rose Worksheet

3. Stroke on front petals of bowl.

4. Stroke on side and center petals.

5. Shade center of bowl, outside of bowl,
and underneath overlapping petals.

6. Shade behind individual rows of petals
on back and front of bowl.

7. Stroke on inside filler petals.

8. Dab center of throat.

(continued from page 91)

8. Using a double-loaded flat paintbrush, stroke in all filler petals with Marigold and White—with White edge of paintbrush toward outside of petals.

9. Using liner brush, dab rose center with Eucalyptus.

Rose Leaves

1. Refer to Rose Leaf Worksheet below. Using a flat paintbrush, base-coat leaves with Eucalyptus + White.

2. Mix Eucalyptus and White to a darker color than the base-coat. Using flat paintbrush, shade leaves and float veins with mixture.

3. Using flat paintbrush, apply retarder medium onto one leaf at a time. Using flat paintbrush, highlight leaf with White + Eucalyptus. Repeat for remaining leaves.

4. Using flat paintbrush, apply retarder medium onto one leaf at a time. Using flat paintbrush, tint leaf with Marigold and then with Butterscotch. Soften, using mop paintbrush. Repeat for remaining leaves.

5. Using scroller paintbrush, add veins, stems, and lay-down strokes onto leaves with Eucalyptus.

Assembly:

1. Using scroll saw, cut two 10" pieces and two 32" pieces from 2" x 4" board to make supports for the seat.

2. Using power drill, predrill all screw holes. Attach 32" pieces with four wood screws each, centered and at same height from ground, along the inside length of the headboard and footboard.

3. To connect the headboard to the footboard, attach the ends of 10" pieces with two wood screws per end at each end of the long supports.

4. Place the seat on the supports and attach it with four wood screws along each length.

5. Fill holes with wood filler and touch-up paint.

Finish:

1. Using 2" chip paintbrush, apply several coats exterior water-based satin varnish, following manufacturer's instructions.

Rose Leaf Worksheet

1. Base-coat, shade, and create veins.

2. Highlight.

3. Strengthen shades.

4. Tint.

5. Vein.

Wood-burned Trout Table

Materials

Painting Surface:
Wooden table: 34" x 24" x
   28" high

Acrylic Paints:
D: Autumn Brown
A: Avocado
D: Black
D: Burnt Sienna
D: Burnt Umber
A: Celery Green
A: Evergreen
A: French Grey Blue
F: Green Umber Artist
   Pigment
A: Grey Sky
A: Hauser Medium Green
A: Honey Brown
A: Mink Tan
A: Olive Yellow
D: Prussian Blue
D: Quaker Grey
L: True Red
D. Wedgwood Blue
D: White

Paintbrushes:
Assorted flats
Assorted mops
Liner
Scroller
Small round
Stencil

Supplies:
Black transfer paper
Disposable foam plates
   for varnish
Embossed metal trout (2)
Exterior spray primer
Exterior water-based
   satin varnish
Palette
Palette knife
Paper towels
Plastic-coated heavy wire
Power drill and ⅛" bit
Retarder medium
Silicone glue
Small clamps
Stylus
Towel
Water container
Wood burner and tips
Wool pad applicator

I found this table at a local thrift store. We had a new pine top made and added decorative molding. What a perfect addition to my husband's den.

Instructions

Note: When making each wash, use two parts paint to one part water unless otherwise noted.

Surface Preparation:
1. Refer to Surface Preparation on pages 15–16.

2. Determine placement of design and transfer Wood-burned Trout Table Patterns on pages 136–137 onto surface.

3. Using wood burner and a fine tip, wood-burn all pattern lines into surface.

4. Mix a wash of each of the following colors: Avocado, Celery Green, and Evergreen.

5. Dampen wool pad applicator with water. Blot excess water onto a towel until applicator is only slightly damp.

6. Using large flat brush, randomly apply each of the color washes onto the reed and cattail area of the table until completely painted. Soften and blend colors by pouncing damp applicator up and down over the area. Allow to dry. Repeat until opaque.

7. Mix a wash of each of the following colors: Prussian Blue and Wedgwood Blue.

8. Using large flat paintbrush, apply wash of Wedgwood Blue onto the water area over the trout and grasses. While still wet randomly streak with wash of Prussian Blue to create the look of water. Allow to dry.

1. Shade behind reeds and cattails.

5. Highlight reeds. Strengthen shading where needed.

2. Base-coat cattails and stems.

3. 1st shade on cattails.

4. 2nd shade on cattails.

Reed & Cattail Worksheet

Paint:
1. Refer to Basic Painting Techniques on pages 11–15.

Reeds & Cattails
1. Refer to Reed & Cattail Worksheet above. Using flat paintbrush, shade behind each reed and where one overlaps another with Green Umber Artist Pigment.

2. Mix a wash of Green Umber Artist Pigment. Using flat paintbrush, apply wash onto all reeds in the very back of the design—even if they are only partial reeds.

3. Using flat paintbrush, apply retarder medium onto reed area of table. Using flat paintbrush, highlight reeds with Celery Green. Soften, using a mop brush.

4. Using flat paintbrush, base-coat cattails with Mink Tan.

5. Using flat paintbrush, apply retarder medium onto one cattail at a time. Using flat paintbrush, shade outside edges with Burnt Sienna. Soften toward the center, using a mop brush. Note: Do not loose the highlight through the middle of the cattail. Repeat for remaining cattails.

6. Using flat paintbrush, apply retarder medium onto one cattail at a time. Using flat paintbrush, shade outside edges with Burnt Umber. Soften, using mop paintbrush. Note: Do not soften out as far as the Burnt Sienna. Repeat for remaining cattails.

7. Using small round paintbrush, base-coat stems and stem spikes with Burnt Umber.

Water Foliage

1. Refer to Water Foliage Worksheet below. Using small round paintbrush, base-coat large leaves in the water area with Olive Yellow until opaque. Using flat paintbrush, shade each leaf with Evergreen.

2. Using small round paintbrush, paint one-stroke leaves with Hauser Medium Green stroked through a puddle of Celery Green so that two colors are present on the brush.

Large Trout

1. Refer to Trout Worksheet below and on page 98. Using flat paintbrush, base-coat trout body with Grey Sky.

2. Using flat paintbrush, base-coat tail and two top fins with Quaker Grey.

3. Using flat paintbrush, base-coat fin on body and two bottom fins with Mink Tan.

(continued on page 99)

Water Foliage Worksheet

1. Base-coat large leaves.

2. Shade large leaves.

3. Paint one-stroke leaves.

Trout Worksheet

1. Base-coat body, tail, fins, and eye. Shade tail, fins, and gills.

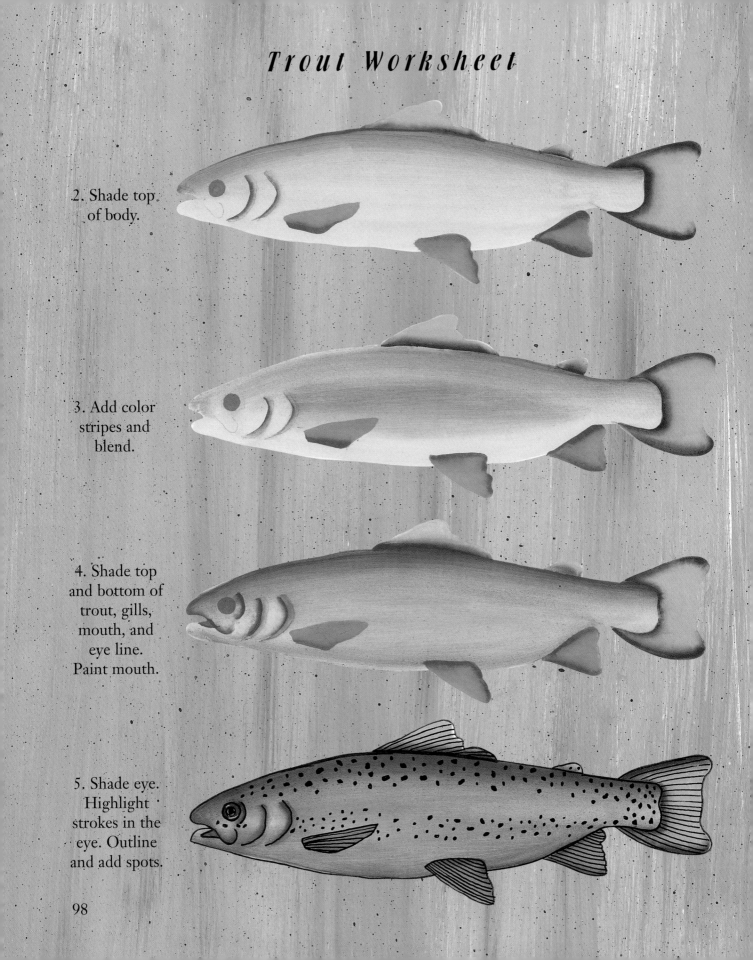

2. Shade top of body.

3. Add color stripes and blend.

4. Shade top and bottom of trout, gills, mouth, and eye line. Paint mouth.

5. Shade eye. Highlight strokes in the eye. Outline and add spots.

(continued from page 97)

4. Using flat paintbrush, base-coat iris of eye with Honey Brown and pupil with Black.

5. Using flat paintbrush, shade tail fin, two top fins, and left side of first gill lines with Quaker Grey + Black.

6. Using flat paintbrush, shade top fins, fin on body, and right side of first gill lines with Autumn Brown.

7. Using flat paintbrush, apply retarder medium onto trout body. Using flat paintbrush, shade top with a wide float of Autumn Brown. Soften, using large mop paintbrush.

8. Using flat paintbrush, apply retarder medium onto trout body. Using round paintbrush, paint a stripe through center of body with True Red. Soften using a mop brush to feather out all edges.

9. Using flat paintbrush, apply retarder medium onto trout body. Using small round paintbrush, paint a stripe just below red stripe with French Grey Blue. Soften and feather out all edges, using mop paintbrush.

10. Using flat paintbrush, apply retarder medium onto trout body. Using small round paintbrush, paint a stripe the length of the trout on the top and bottom of the body with Quaker Grey. Soften into the body, using mop paintbrush.

11. Using flat paintbrush, apply retarder medium onto trout body. Using small round paintbrush, paint a stripe to top length of the trout with Quaker Grey + Black. Soften into the body, using mop paintbrush. Note: Take care to avoid completely covering previous shading.

12. Using flat paintbrush, shade line behind eye, mouth line, and inside of mouth with Quaker Grey + Black.

13. Using flat paintbrush, shade around outside edge of iris with Autumn Brown. Using liner paintbrush, paint highlight strokes on eye with White.

Metal Trout

1. Apply several light coats exterior spray primer onto metal trout, following manufacturer's instructions, until well covered. Allow to dry 24 hours.

2. Paint metal trout, following instructions for Large Trout on pages 97–99.

Finish:

1. Using scroller paintbrush, outline everything that is wood-burned with thinned Black.

2. Using small round paintbrush, fill in spots on trout body with Black.

3. Using stencil paintbrush, fly-speck entire table top and metal trout with thinned Black.

4. Using large flat paintbrush, paint table sides, bottom, and legs with Black.

5. Using flat paintbrush, apply several coats of exterior water-based satin varnish to table and metal trout.

Assembly:

1. Using power drill and ⅛" drill bit, drill hole in each table leg on the front of the table to hold wire.

2. Glue each metal trout onto one wire end. Clamp until dry.

3. Bend wire to represent waves.

4. Place a small amount of glue on the remaining wire end and insert into the hole in table leg.

Materials

Painting Surface:
Wooden bench: 42" x 11"
   x 17" high
Wrought-iron headboard:
   twin size

Acrylic Paints:
A: Bittersweet Chocolate
D: Bittersweet Orange
D: Black
A: Black Green
L: Burnt Umber
A: Cadmium Orange
A: Deep Periwinkle
D: Denim Blue
A: Golden Straw
A: Hauser Dark Green
A: Hauser Light Green
A: Hauser Medium Green
D: Leaf Green
A: Lemon Yellow
A: Light Buttermilk
D: Magnolia White
F: Medium Yellow
A: Napa Red
D: Poppy Orange
A: Royal Fuchsia
A: Snow White
D: Soft Grey
A: Terra Cotta
D: Trail Tan
D: White

Brushes:
Assorted flats
Chip: 2"
Filbert
Liner

Supplies:
Black transfer paper
Cheesecloth
Decoupage medium
Disposable foam bowls
   for mixing paint
Disposable foam plates
   for varnish
Exterior satin paint:
   periwinkle
Exterior spray primer
Exterior water-based satin
   varnish
Foam paint roller
Natural sea sponge
Palette
Palette knife
Paper towels
Power sander and sand-
   paper
Scallop-edged scissors
Stylus
Tack cloth
Water container
Water-based glaze
   medium
Water-based wood primer
Watercolor paper: 140
   hot press
White transfer paper

This iron headboard was the perfect backboard for a bench. Made of wood, the bench is slightly longer than the headboard and has a 2" x 4" standard at each end for attaching it with screws. The poppies and stamps were inspired by the design on a postcard.

Instructions

Designed by: Yvonne Heiner

Surface Preparation:

1. Refer to Surface Preparation on pages 15–16.

2. Using power sander, sand bench to prepare it to be painted. Using tack cloth, wipe off any sawdust.

3. Using foam paint roller, apply water-based wood primer onto bench, following manufacturer's instructions.

4. Apply several light coats exterior spray primer onto headboard, following manufacturer's instructions, until well covered. Allow to dry 24 hours.

5. Using foam paint roller for bench and natural sea sponge for headboard, base-coat each with periwinkle exterior satin paint. Allow to dry.

6. In disposable bowl, mix one half part periwinkle exterior satin paint and one half part White to one part glaze medium.

7. Using natural sea sponge, apply mixture onto bench and headboard. Soften and blend the sponging, using a rolled piece of cheesecloth.

8. Determine placement of motifs, then transfer Poppies Bench Pattern on page 138 onto bench surface with black transfer paper.

Poppy Worksheet

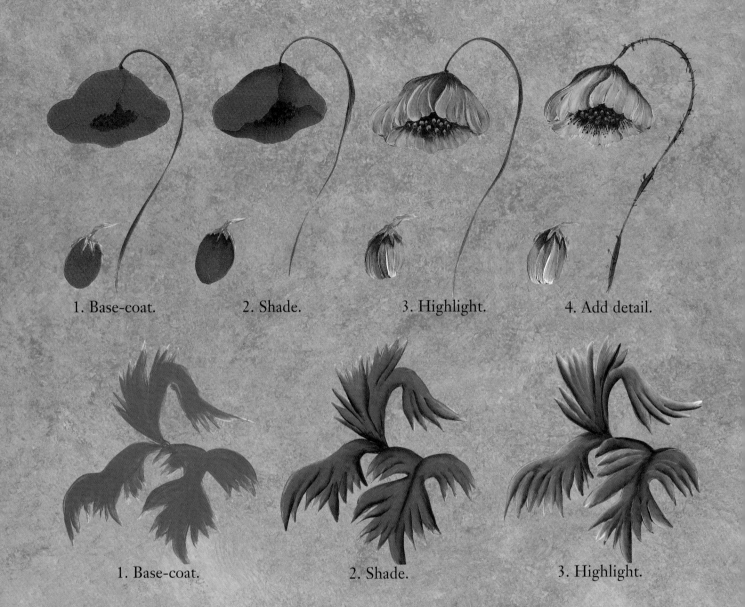

1. Base-coat. 2. Shade. 3. Highlight. 4. Add detail.

1. Base-coat. 2. Shade. 3. Highlight.

Paint:

1. Refer to Basic Painting Techniques on pages 11–15.

Poppies

1. Refer to Poppy Worksheet above. Using flat paintbrush, base-coat every other poppy with Lemon Yellow, Poppy Orange, or Royal Fuchsia.

2. Using flat paintbrush, base-coat poppy centers with Bittersweet Chocolate.

3. Using flat paintbrush, shade each poppy as follows: for Lemon Yellow poppy, shade with Cadmium Orange; for Poppy Orange poppy, shade with Cadmium Orange + Napa Red; for Royal Fuchsia poppy, shade with Napa Red.

4. Refer to Stroke Diagram on page 138. Using filbert paintbrush, highlight each poppy with comma strokes as follows: for Lemon Yellow poppy, highlight with Snow White tipped with Cadmium Orange; for Poppy Orange poppy highlight with Medium Yellow, tipped with Cadmium Orange; for Royal Fuchsia poppy, highlight with Snow White tipped with Napa Red.

5. Using flat paintbrush, shade poppy centers with Black.

6. Using flat paintbrush, paint small C-Strokes here and there with Golden Straw to highlight top of poppy center.

Poppy Leaves

1. Refer to Poppy Worksheet on opposite page. Using flat paintbrush, base-coat all leaves and stems with Leaf Green.

2. Using flat paintbrush, shade dark recesses and behind any overlapping leaf with Black Green.

3. Using flat paintbrush, highlight all light areas with Medium Yellow.

Ferns & Stems

1. Using liner paintbrush, stroke on some ferns with thinned Leaf Green and some with thinned Black Green. Note: Try stroking on some with a mixture of the two paints.

2. Using a liner paintbrush, pull on stems with Black Green. Paint some tiny lines coming out from main stem to make it look furry.

Stamps

1. Transfer Poppies Bench Stamp Patterns on page 139 onto watercolor paper with black transfer paper.

2. Using scallop-edged scissors, cut out Australia stamp. Using craft scissors, cut out Airmail stamp.

3. Using flat paintbrush, base-coat Airmail stamp with Denim Blue. Allow to dry. Transfer stars and airmail words onto painted stamp with white transfer paper.

4. Using flat and liner paintbrushes, paint stars and words with Light Buttermilk until opaque.

5. Refer to Butterfly Worksheet on page 104. Using flat paintbrush, base-coat wings of open-winged butterfly on Australia stamp with Deep Periwinkle.

6. Using flat paintbrush, base-coat wings of hanging butterfly with Bittersweet Orange.

7. Using flat paintbrush, base-coat butterfly body with Trail Tan.

8. Mix a wash of Terra Cotta. Using flat paintbrush, apply wash onto twig.

9. Using liner paintbrush, outline open-winged butterfly with Black.

10. Using liner paintbrush, add lines and spots onto wings of both butterflies with Soft Grey.

11. Using flat paintbrush, shade around all edges of wings and bottom of each butterfly body with Burnt Umber.

12. Using flat paintbrush, shade along inside of wings and next to body on open-winged butterfly with Burnt Umber.

13. Using flat paintbrush, highlight over lines and spots of hanging butterfly and body of open-winged butterfly with Magnolia White.

14. Using flat paintbrush, shade twig with Terra Cotta.

15. Using liner paintbrush, add lines onto twig to look like pine needles with Hauser Dark Green, Hauser Light Green, and Hauser Medium Green.

16. Using liner paintbrush, paint letters and numbers with Black.

104

Butterfly Worksheet

1. Base-coat and outline.

2. Add lines and spots to wings.

3. Shade body and around edges of wings.

4. Shade inside of wings and next to body.

5. Highlight lines and spots.

6. Add lines for pine needles.

Finish:

1. Using large flat paintbrush, adhere stamps onto bench with decoupage medium, following manufacturer's instructions.

2. Using 2" chip paintbrush, apply three coats exterior water-based satin varnish over bench, following manufacturer's instructions.

Patio Storage Cabinet

Materials

Painting Surface:
Old file cabinet:
   29" x 18" x 34" high

Acrylic Paints:
A: Antique Teal
D: Autumn Brown
D: Black
D: Bridgeport Grey
D: Burnt Sienna
F: Buttercream
A: Celery Green
D: Chocolate Cherry
D: Cinnamon
D: Dark Foliage
D: Dark Goldenrod
A: Deep Periwinkle
L: Dusty Green
D: Dusty Purple
A: Honey Brown
F: Indigo
D: Lavender
A: Moon Yellow
A: Neutral Grey
F: Night Sky
D: Oasis Green
D: Old Parchment
A: Olde Gold
A: Olive Green
A: Plantation Pine
D: Poppy Orange
F: Raw Sienna Pure
   Pigment
D: Red Iron Oxide
D: Rhythm 'N Blue
A: Silver Sage Green
D: Soft Grey
D: Timberline Green
D: White
A: Wisteria

Paintbrushes:
Assorted flats
Filbert
Liner
Scroller
Small round

Supplies:
Black transfer paper
Clean soft rags
Disposable foam bowls for
   mixing paint
Exterior satin spray
   varnish
Exterior spray paint:
   almond
Exterior spray primer
Painter's tape: blue
Palette
Palette knife
Paper towels
Permanent marker: black
Rubber stamps: oriental
   writing
Ruler
Sandpaper
Soap
Stamp pad: black
Stylus
Tack cloth
Water container
Wool pad applicators:
   large; small

I found this filing cabinet at a thrift store for a clearance price of $5. What a perfect item to store patio dishes, cutlery, and assorted linens for patio dinners and entertaining.

Instructions

See photos on pages 6–7 and 105.

Note: When making each wash, use one part paint to two parts water.

Surface Preparation:

1. Refer to Surface Preparation on pages 15–16.

2. Wash cabinet thoroughly with soap and water. Allow to dry.

3. Apply several light coats exterior spray primer onto cabinet, following manufacturer's instructions. Allow to dry 24 hours.

4. Lightly sand the painting area to smooth painting surface. Using tack cloth, wipe off any dust.

5. Apply several coats almond exterior spray paint onto cabinet, following manufacturer's instructions. Allow to dry 24 hours.

6. In disposable bowls, mix a wash of Dusty Green, a wash of Old Parchment, and a wash of Lavender.

7. Dampen large wool pad applicator with water. Blot excess water onto a towel until applicator is only slightly damp. Randomly brush each of the color washes directly onto applicator.

8. Randomly apply color washes onto one side

of cabinet, pouncing applicator up and down over surface to soften and mottle colors. Note: If more color is needed in an area, reapply color washes where needed. Soften, using applicator. Allow to dry.

9. Repeat Steps 7–8 on remaining sides and top. Allow to dry.

10. Determine what size squares would best suit your cabinet by measuring its width and length. (Squares shown are 4" x 4".) Tape off one side of cabinet with blue painter's tape.

11. Refer to Squares Legend below. Choose color combinations from legend and apply to squares, following instructions in Steps 6–8 and using the smaller wool pad applicator.

Squares Legend

Square #1:	Autumn Brown
	Wisteria
	White
Square #2:	Autumn Brown
	Wisteria
Square #3:	Wisteria
	Dusty Purple
Square #4:	Wisteria
	Olive Green
Square #5:	Wisteria
	White
Square #6:	Dusty Purple
	Olive Green

12. Remove tape and repeat Steps 10–11 for remaining sides and top. Note: Leave some squares the original finish.

13. Determine placement of flowers, then

transfer Patio Storage Cabinet Patterns on page 140 onto surface within tiles.

Paint:
1. Refer to Basic Painting Techniques on pages 11–15.

Pompon #1
1. Refer to Pompon Worksheet on page 108. Using flat paintbrush, base-coat light portion of pompon with Olde Gold.

2. Using flat paintbrush, base-coat dark portion of pompon with Indigo.

3. Using flat paintbrush, shade behind each petal on light portion of pompon with Indigo.

4. Using flat paintbrush, shade behind each petal on dark portion of pompon with Indigo + Black.

5. Using scroller paintbrush, stroke fine lines onto each Olde Gold petal with Olde Gold + White.

6. Add more White to mixture in Step 5. Using scroller paintbrush, stroke fine lines onto each

Pompon Worksheet

1. Base-coat and shade.

2. Highlight lines.

3. 2nd highlight lines.

4. Base-coat center and add dots.
Shade to define petals.

5. Highlight dots on center.
Highlight strokes where needed.

petal to highlight where needed for more intensity.

7. Using scroller paintbrush, stroke fine lines onto each Indigo petal with Indigo + White.

8. Add more White to mixture in Step 7. Using scroller paintbrush, stroke fine lines onto petals to further highlight.

9. Using flat paintbrush, base-coat pompon center with Neutral Grey.

10. Using stylus, dot pompon center with Indigo.

11. Using liner paintbrush, highlight pompon center with a smaller dot of White + Indigo.

Pompon #2
1. Refer to Pompon Worksheet above. Using flat paintbrush, base-coat light portion of pompon with Olde Gold.

2. Using flat paintbrush, base-coat dark portion of pompon with Dark Goldenrod.

3. Using flat paintbrush, shade behind each petal on light portion of pompon with Indigo.

4. Using flat paintbrush, shade behind each petal on dark portion of pompon with Burnt Sienna.

5. Using scroller paintbrush, stroke fine lines onto each Olde Gold petal with Olde Gold + White.

6. Add more White to mixture in Step 5. Using scroller paintbrush, stroke fine lines onto each petal to highlight where needed for more intensity.

7. Using scroller paintbrush, stroke fine lines onto each Dark Goldenrod petal with Dark Goldenrod + White.

108

8. Add more White to mixture in Step 7. Using scroller paintbrush, stroke fine lines onto petals to further highlight.

9. Using flat paintbrush, base-coat pompon center with Neutral Grey.

10. Using stylus, dot pompon center with Dark Goldenrod.

11. Using liner paintbrush, highlight pompon center with a smaller dot of White + Dark Goldenrod.

Pompon #3

1. Refer to Pompon Worksheet on opposite page. Using flat paintbrush, base-coat light portion of pompon with Olde Gold.

2. Using flat paintbrush, base-coat dark portion of pompon with Antique Teal + a little Black.

3. Using flat paintbrush, shade behind each petal on light portion of pompon with Indigo.

4. Using flat paintbrush, shade behind each petal on dark portion of pompon with Antique Teal + Black.

5. Using scroller paintbrush, stroke fine lines onto each Olde Gold petal with Olde Gold + White.

6. Add more White to mixture in Step 5. Using scroller paintbrush, stroke fine lines onto each petal to highlight where needed for more intensity.

7. Using scroller paintbrush, stroke fine lines onto each Antique Teal petal with Antique Teal + White.

8. Add more White to mixture in Step 7. Using scroller paintbrush, stroke fine lines onto petals to further highlight.

9. Using flat paintbrush, base-coat pompon center with Neutral Grey.

10. Using stylus, dot pompon center with Antique Teal.

11. Using liner paintbrush, highlight pompon center with a smaller dot of Antique Teal + White.

Pompon Flower #4

1. Refer to Pompon Worksheet on opposite page. Using flat paintbrush, base-coat light portion of pompon with Dark Goldenrod.

2. Using flat paintbrush, base-coat dark portion of pompon with Chocolate Cherry + a little White.

3. Using flat paintbrush, shade behind each petal on light portion of pompon with Chocolate Cherry.

4. Using flat paintbrush, shade behind each petal on dark portion of pompon with Chocolate Cherry + Black.

5. Using scroller paintbrush, stroke fine lines onto each Dark Goldenrod petal with Dark Goldenrod + White.

6. Add more White to mixture in Step 5. Using scroller paintbrush, stroke fine lines onto each petal to highlight where needed for more intensity.

7. Using scroller paintbrush, stroke fine lines onto each Chocolate Cherry petal with Chocolate Cherry + White.

8. Add more White to mixture in Step 7. Using scroller paintbrush, stroke fine lines onto petals to further highlight.

9. Using flat paintbrush, base-coat pompon center with Neutral Grey.

10. Using stylus, dot pompon center with Burnt Sienna.

11. Using liner paintbrush, highlight pompon center with a smaller dot of Dark Goldenrod + White.

Pompon #5

1. Refer to Pompon Worksheet on page 108. Using flat paintbrush, base-coat entire pompon with Dark Goldenrod.

2. Using flat paintbrush, shade behind each petal with Burnt Sienna.

3. Using flat paintbrush, shade where needed with Cinnamon.

4. Using scroller paintbrush, stroke fine lines onto each petal with Dark Goldenrod + White.

5. Add more White to mixture in Step 4. Using scroller paintbrush, stroke fine lines onto each petal to highlight where needed for more intensity.

6. Using flat paintbrush, base-coat pompon center with Neutral Grey.

7. Using stylus, dot pompon center with Cinnamon.

8. Using liner paintbrush, highlight pompon center with a smaller dot of Dark Goldenrod.

Pompon Leaf #1

1. Refer to Pompon Leaf Worksheet at right. Using flat paintbrush, base-coat leaf with Plantation Pine.

2. Using flat paintbrush, shade leaf with Indigo.

3. Using flat paintbrush, highlight and vein leaf with Olde Gold.

Pompon Leaf #2

1. Refer to Pompon Leaf Worksheet below. Using flat paintbrush, base-coat leaf with Dark Foliage.

2. Using flat paintbrush, shade leaf with Indigo.

3. Using flat paintbrush, highlight and vein leaf with Dusty Green.

Pompon Leaf #3

1. Refer to Pompon Leaf Worksheet below. Using flat paintbrush, base-coat leaf with Dark Goldenrod + Burnt Sienna + Poppy Orange.

2. Using flat paintbrush, shade leaf with Chocolate Cherry.

3. Using flat paintbrush, highlight leaf with Dark Goldenrod.

4. Using flat paintbrush, vein leaf with Dark Goldenrod + a little White.

Pompon Leaf Worksheet

1. Base-coat and shade.   2. Highlight.

3. Vein.

Ray Flower Worksheet

1. Base-coat and shade.

2. Highlight petals.

3. Line petals.

4. Lighter lines on petals.

Dark Yellow Ray Flowers

1. Refer to Ray Flower Worksheet above. Using flat paintbrush, base-coat each flower and bud with Dark Goldenrod.

2. Using flat paintbrush, shade where one petal overlaps another with Cinnamon.

3. Using flat paintbrush, paint flower center with Cinnamon.

4. Using flat paintbrush, highlight all petals with Old Parchment.

5. Using scroller paintbrush, line all petals with Butter Cream.

Light Yellow Ray Flowers

1. Refer to Ray Flower Worksheet above. Using flat paintbrush, base-coat each flower and bud with Moon Yellow.

2. Using flat paintbrush, shade where one petal overlaps another with Honey Brown.

3. Using flat paintbrush, paint flower center with Honey Brown.

4. Using flat paintbrush, highlight all petals with Old Parchment.

5. Using scroller paintbrush, line all petals with Butter Cream.

Purple Ray Flower

1. Refer to Ray Flower Worksheet above. Using flat paintbrush, base-coat each flower and bud with Wisteria.

2. Using flat paintbrush, shade where one petal overlaps another with Chocolate Cherry.

3. Using flat paintbrush, paint flower center with Chocolate Cherry.

4. Using flat paintbrush, highlight all petals with Soft Grey.

5. Using scroller paintbrush, line all petals with Soft Grey + a little White.

6. Using flat paintbrush, paint bud calyx with Dusty Green + Dark Foliage.

111

Ray Flower Leaves

1. Refer to Ray Flower Leaf Worksheet at right. Using double-loaded filbert paintbrush, stroke on leaves with Dark Foliage and Dusty Green.

2. Using a scroller paintbrush, stroke on all stems with Dark Foliage + Dusty Green.

Fanciful Stroke Flowers

1. Refer to Fanciful Stroke Flower Worksheet at right. Using double-loaded filbert paintbrush, stroke on flowers with Moon Yellow and Dark Goldenrod with Moon Yellow toward outside of flower. Note: They may take two coats to cover.

2. Using liner paintbrush, paint strokes around each flower from the outside edge in with Moon Yellow + White.

3. Using liner paintbrush, paint center strokes with Raw Sienna.

4. Using stylus, paint dots on center with Moon Yellow + White.

5. Using scroller paintbrush, paint all stems with Dark Foliage.

Blue Clover Leaves

1. Refer to Clover Leaf Worksheet on opposite page. Using small round paintbrush, base-coat each leaf Rhythm 'N Blue.

Ray Flower Leaf Worksheet

1. Beginning strokes.   2. 2nd strokes.   3. Filler strokes.

Fanciful Stroke Flower Worksheet

1. Double-load and stroke on flowers.

2. Highlight strokes.

3. Stroke and dot centers. Add stems.

2. Using flat paintbrush, shade one side of each leaf and vein with Night Sky.

3. Using flat paintbrush, highlight vein and remaining side of each leaf with Deep Periwinkle.

4. Using scroller paintbrush, paint each stem with Rhythm 'N Blue.

Green Clover Leaves
1. Refer to Clover Leaf Worksheet at right. Using small round paintbrush, base-coat each leaf with Timberline Green.

2. Using flat paintbrush, shade one side of each leaf and vein with Plantation Pine.

3. Using flat paintbrush, highlight vein and remaining side of each leaf with Celery Green.

4. Using scroller paintbrush, paint each stem with Timberline Green.

Light Green Clover Leaves
1. Refer to Clover Leaf Worksheet at right. Using small round paintbrush, base-coat each leaf with Oasis Green.

2. Using flat paintbrush, shade one side of each leaf and vein with Dusty Green.

3. Using flat paintbrush, highlight vein and remaining side of each leaf with Silver Sage Green.

4. Using scroller paintbrush, paint each stem with Oasis Green.

White Clover Leaves
1. Refer to Clover Leaf Worksheet at right. Using small round paintbrush, base-coat each leaf with Soft Grey.

2. Using flat paintbrush, shade one side of each leaf and vein with Bridgeport Grey.

3. Using flat paintbrush, highlight vein and remaining side of each leaf with White.

4. Using flat paintbrush, paint each stem with Soft Grey.

Filler Fern Leaves
1. Using small round paintbrush, base-coat stroke on each leaf and stem with Red Iron Oxide.

Finish:
1. Using permanent black marker, line each square.

2. Apply rubber stamp designs where desired.

3. Using liner paintbrush, paint some swirls onto several of the colored squares with White.

4. Using liner paintbrush, paint a series of three strokes onto some squares.

5. Apply several coats exterior satin spray varnish, following manufacturer's instructions.

Clover Leaf Worksheet

1. Base-coat.   3. Highlight.

2. Shade.   4. Add stems. Vein.

Rustic Morning Glory Birdhouse Patterns

pages 18–22

Enlarge pattern 170% for actual size
of painted sample.

Enlarge pattern 250% for actual size
of painted sample.

Enlarge pattern 170% for actual size
of painted sample.

Faux Tile Table
Large Fruit
Patterns

pages 23–29

Enlarge patterns 145% for actual size of painted sample.

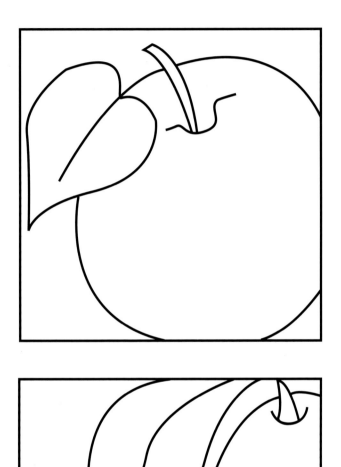

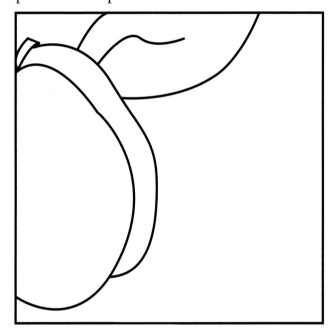

Oversized Grapes Chair Pattern

pages 30–32

Enlarge pattern 165% for actual size of painted sample.

Oversized Strawberries Chair Pattern

p a g e s   3 3 – 3 5

Enlarge pattern 145% for actual size of painted sample.

Faux Tile Table
Small Fruit Patterns
pages 23–25 & 36–39

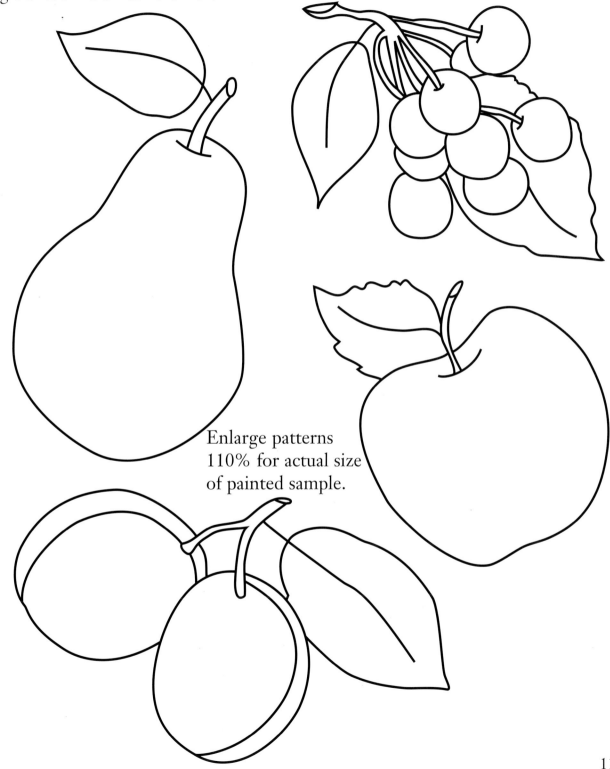

Enlarge patterns
110% for actual size
of painted sample.

Geranium Planter Pattern

pages 40–44

Enlarge pattern 155% for actual size
of painted sample.

Folk Art Tables Pattern

pages 45–49

Enlarge pattern 210% for actual size of painted sample.

Flowered Washstand
Birdbath Patterns
pages 50–53

Enlarge patterns 165% for actual size
of painted sample.

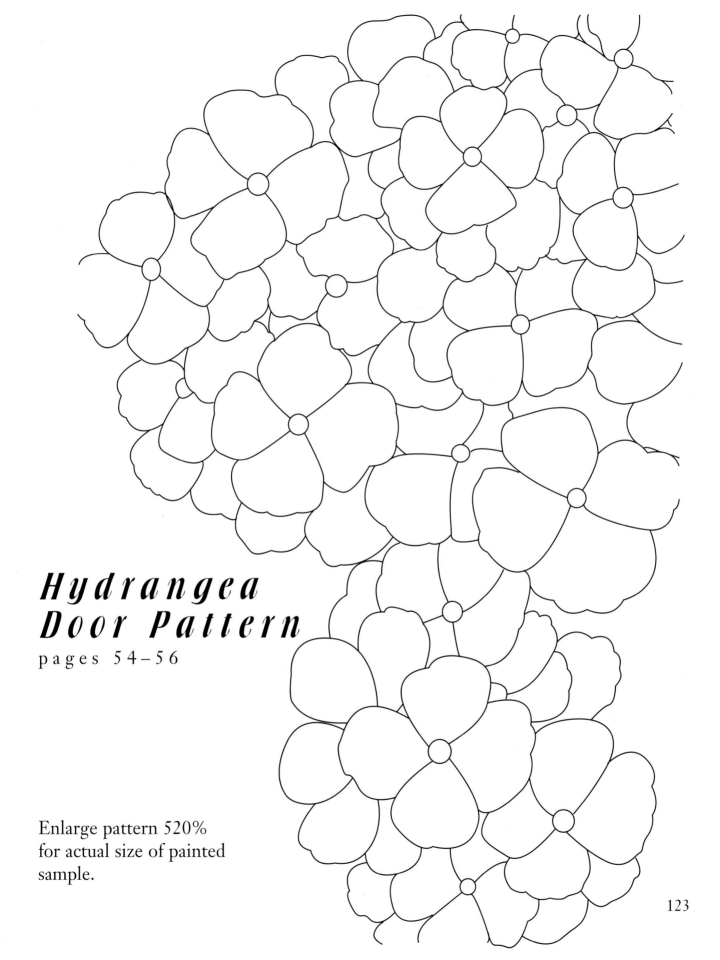

Hydrangea
Door Pattern
pages 54–56

Enlarge pattern 520%
for actual size of painted
sample.

123

Angel Trumpet Potting Table Patterns

pages 57–61

Enlarge patterns 255% for actual size
of painted sample.

Tulip Pedestal Pattern

pages 62–66

Enlarge pattern 400% for actual size of painted sample.

Enlarge pattern 200% for actual size of painted sample.

Second-hand Chic Table Patterns

pages 67–73

Patterns are actual size of painted sample.

Enlarge pattern 140% for actual size
of painted sample.

Enlarge patterns 125% for actual
size of painted sample.

Second-hand Chic Table Pattern

pages 67–73

Pattern is actual size of painted sample.

Autumn Leaves Hutch Patterns

pages 74–77

Patterns are actual size of painted sample.

Gaillardia & Dahlia Washtubs Pattern

pages 82–88

Enlarge pattern 145% for actual size of painted sample.

Romantic Roses
Bench Pattern

pages 89–93

Pattern is actual size of painted sample.

Romantic Roses
Stencil Pattern

pages 89–93

Enlarge pattern 125%
for actual size of painted
sample.

Wood-burned Trout Table Patterns

pages 94–99

Enlarge patterns 340% for actual size of painted sample.

Poppies Bench Pattern

pages 100–104

Stroke Diagram

 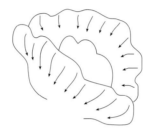 

Enlarge pattern 410% for actual size
of painted sample.

Poppies Bench Stamp Patterns

pages 100–104

AIR MAIL

P A R A V I O N

Australia Post

Enlarge patterns
110% for actual
size of painted
sample.

Australia   80c

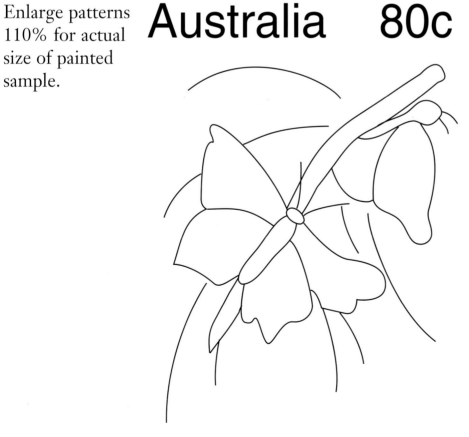

Patio Storage Cabinet Patterns

pages 105–113

Enlarge patterns 140% for actual size of painted sample.

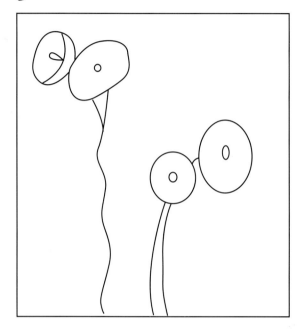

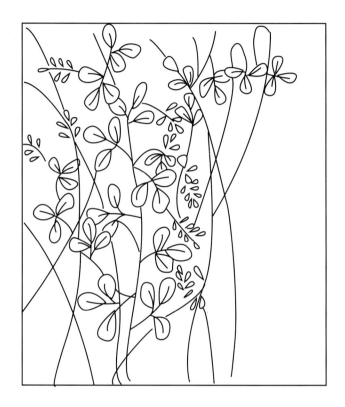

Paint Conversion Chart

D: Delta	F: Folkart	A: Americana	L: Aleene's
Autumn Brown	Nutmeg	Milk Chocolate	Burnt Umber + Yellow Ochre
Bahama Purple	Night Sky + White	Deep Periwinkle	Medium Lavender
Bittersweet Orange	Tangerine	Tangerine	True Apricot
Black	Licorice	Lamp Black	Black
Black Cherry	Burgundy	Napa Red, Alizarin Crimson	Deep Mauve
Black Green	Wrought Iron	Black Green	Black + Hunter Green
Bridgeport Grey	Whipped Berry	Slate Gray	Black + White
Bungalow Blue			
Burnt Sienna	Burnt Sierra	Terra Cotta+ Burnt Orange	Deep Peach
Burnt Umber	Burnt Umber	Dark Chocolate	Deep Blush + Black
Chocolate Cherry	Dioxazine Purple + Burnt Umber	Black Plum	Dusty Fuchsia + Black
Cinnamon	Huckleberry	Rookwood	True Red + Burnt Umber
Crocus Yellow	Medium Yellow + Turner's Yellow	Cadmium Yellow	True Yellow + True Orange
Dark Brown	Maple Syrup	Dark Chocolate	Deep Blush + Black
Dark Foliage	Hunter Green	Forest Green	Deep Green
Dark Forest Green	Thicket	Plan Pine	Dusty Sage + Black
Dark Goldenrod	Burnt Sienna + Tangerine	Cadmium Orange + Antique Gold	True Orange + Burnt Umber
Dark Jungle	Green Meadow	Avocado + Burnt Umber	Deep Sage
Denim Blue	Blue Ribbon	Blue Violet + Cool Neutral	True Blue
Dunes Beige	Capp + White	Cashmere Beige + White	White + Dusty Beige
Dusty Purple	Plum Chiffon	Plum	Dusty Fuchsia
Eucalyptus			
G. P. Purple	White + Dioxazine Purple	White + Dioxazine Purple	Deep Violet + White
Grey Sky			
Lavender	White + Dioxazine Purple	Lavender + White	Dusty Violet + White
Leaf Green	Fresh Foliage, Hauser Light Green	Hauser Light Green	True Lime + Deep Sage
Lichen Grey	Barn Wood	Driftwood	True Grey + Wicker
Light Foliage	Hauser Light Green	Hauser Light Green	Deep Sage + Medium Yellow
Magnolia White	Wicker White	White Wash	White
Medium Foliage	Hauser Medium Green	Hauser Medium Green	Deep Green + Deep Beige
Oasis Green	Poetry Green	Green Mist	Dusty Green + White
Old Parchment	Sunflower	Moon Yellow + White	Yellow Ochre + White
Poppy Orange	Pure Orange + Red Light	Cadmium Orange	True Poppy
Prussian Blue	Prussian Blue	Navy Blue	Deep Blue
Pumpkin	Tangerine + Glazed Carrots	Pumpkin	True Orange
Purple	Dioxazine Purple	Dioxazine Purple	Deep Violet
Quaker Grey	Dove Gray	Grey Sky	True Grey + White
Red Iron Oxide	Light Red Oxide	Georgia Clay	Deep Blush
Rhythm 'N Blue	Night Sky	Blue Violet + Dioxazine Purple	Medium Violet + True Lavender
Rosetta Pink	Peach Perfection	Peach Sherbet	Deep Blush + White
Royal Plum	Purple Passion	Burgundy Wine + True Blue	Dusty Fuchsia + Burnt Umber
Soft Grey	White + Light Grey	Dove Grey + White	White + True Grey
Timberline Green	Southern Pine + Yellow Ochre	Antique Green	Deep Beige + Deep Sage
Trail Tan	Butter Pecan	Khaki Tan	Dusty Beige + Medium Grey
Tuscan Red			
Village Green	Bayberry + White	Mint Julep	White + Deep Green + Burnt Umber
Vintage Wine	Red Violet	Royal Purple	Deep Violet
Wedgwood Blue	French Blue	Williamsburg Blue + White	Dusty Blue + White
White	Titanium White	Titanium White	White
Wisteria	Plum Pudding + White	Plum + White	Dusty Fuchsia

A: Americana	D: Delta	F: Folkart	L: Aleene's
Antique Rose	Tomato Spice + White	Primrose + Light Red Oxide	Deep Mauve + Medium Red
Antique Teal	Blue Spruce	Wintergreen	Dusty Spruce + Deep Spruce
Arbor Green	Alpine	Shamrock + White	Dusty Green
Avocado	Dark Jungle	Green Meadow	Deep Sage
Base Flesh	Normandy Rose	White + Burnt Sienna	Dusty Blush + White
Bittersweet Chocolate	Dark Burnt Umber	Burnt Umber	Burnt Umber + Black
Black Forest Green	Deep River	Hunter Green	Deep Green + Deep Spruce
Black Green	Black Green	Wrought Iron	Dusty Spruce + Black
Black Plum	Chocolate Cherry	Dioxazine Purple + Burnt Umber	Dusty Fuchsia + Black
Buttermilk	Antique White	Tapioca, Warm White	Ivory
Cadmium Orange	Orange, Poppy Orange	Glazed Carrots + Calico Red	True Poppy
Cadmium Yellow	Yellow	School Bus Yellow, Medium Yellow	True Yellow
Celery Green	Stonewedge	Basil Green	Dusty Sage + Medium Grey
Charcoal	Black Green	Wrought Iron	Black + Deep Sage
Dark Chocolate	Burnt Umber	Burnt Umber	Burnt Umber + Black
Deep Midnight Blue	Nightfall, Cadet Blue	Heartland Blue	Deep Blue + Black
Deep Burgundy	Mendo, Barn Red	Burgundy	Deep Mauve
Deep Periwinkle	Ultramarine Blue + White + G. P. Purple	Night Sky + White	Deep Lavender + White
Driftwood	Lichen Grey	Barnwood	Beige + True Grey
Dusty Sage			
Evergreen	Forest Green	Thicket	Deep Green + Burnt Umber
Forest Green	Deep River, Dark Foliage Green	Shamrock, Hunter Green	Deep Green
French Grey Blue	Midnight + White	Settler's Blue	Dusty Blue + Black
Golden Straw	Straw	Buttercup	Yellow Ochre + True Yellow
Gooseberry Pink	Gypsy Rose	Salmon	Deep Blush + Medium Red
Grey Sky	White + Bridgeport	Dove Grey	White + True Grey + Dusty Blue
Hauser Dark Green	Deep River	Hauser Dark Green	Hunter Green
Hauser Light Green	Light Foliage Green	Hauser Light Green	Deep Sage + Medium Yellow
Hauser Medium Green	Chrome Green Light	Hauser Medium Green	Deep Green + Deep Beige
Honey Brown	Golden Brown	English Mustard	Yellow Ochre
Hot Shots Fiery Red			
Hot Shots Red			
Hot Shots Scorching Yellow			
Hot Shots Sizzling Pink			
Hot Shots Thermal Green			
Jade Green	Wedgwood Green	Bayberry, Basil Green	Dusty Sage + Medium Grey
Lemon Yellow	Luscious Lemon	Yellow Light	Medium Yellow
Light Buttermilk	Light Ivory	Ivory White	Ivory
Marigold	Empire Gold	Turners Yellow	Maize
Mauve	Rose Mist	Potpourri Rose	Dusty Mauve + White
Mink Tan	Light Chocolate	Nutmeg + White	Dusty Beige
Mint Julep Green	White + Christmas Green	Shamrock + White	Dusty Green + White
Moon Yellow	Old Parchment	Sunflower	White + True Apricot
Napa Red	Mulberry	Burgundy	Burgundy
Neutral Grey	Hippo Grey	Medium Grey	True Grey + White
Olde Gold	Mustard	Golden Harvest + Clover	Medium Yellow + Deep Khaki
Olive Green	Leaf Green + White	Fresh Foliage + White	Medium Yellow + Deep Sage
Olive Yellow			
Pink Chiffon	Rose Petal Pink	White + Carnation Pink	White + Light Fuchsia
Plantation Pine	English Yew	Southern Pine	Deep Sage
Red Iron Oxide	Red Iron Oxide	Light Red Oxide	Deep Blush + White
Royal Fuchsia	Magenta	Fuchsia	True Fuchsia
Royal Purple	Vintage Wine	Dioxazine Purple + Licorice	Deep Violet + True Grey
Sable Brown	Territorial Beige	Nutmeg + Teddy Bear Brown	Dusty Beige
Sand	Flesh Tan	Taffy + Tapioca	Light Yellow + Beige + White
Silver Sage Green	Silver Pine	White + Green Umber	Dusty Green + Medium Grey + White
Snow White			
Soft Blue	Ocean Blue Blue + White	Sky Blue + White	White + Dusty Spruce
Terra Cotta	Mocha	Buckskin Brown	Deep Peach + Medium Orange
Wisteria	Bahama Purple + Lisa Pink + White	Heather + Coast Blue + White	Light Lavender

F: Folkart	D: Delta	A: Americana	L: Aleene's
Artist Pigment **Green Umber**			
Burnt Carmine	Sonoma + Vintage Wine	Rookwood Red + Dioxazine Purple	Deep Fuchsia + Burnt Umber
Buttercream	Pale Yellow + White	Taffy Cream + White	Light Yellow + White
Butterscotch	Pigskin + Bittersweet	Cadmium Orange + Antique Gold	True Apricot + Deep Peach
Crimson	Napthol Crimson	Berry Red	Holiday Red
Green Forest	Christmas Green	Leaf Green	Deep Green + Hunter Green
Indigo	Blue Storm	Navy Blue + Black	Navy Blue
Medium Yellow	Yellow + White	Cadmium Yellow	True Yellow
Night Sky	Rhythm 'N Blue	Dioxazine Purple + Navy Blue	Deep Lavender + Deep Fuchsia
Payne's Grey	Midnight, Blue Storm	Payne's Grey	Dusty Blue + Black
Purple	Purple	Dioxazine Purple	Deep Violet
Raw Sienna Pure Pigment	Raw Sienna	Terra Cotta	Dusty Peach + True Apricot

L: Aleene's	D: Delta	A: Americana	F: Folkart
Burnt Umber	Brown Iron Oxide	Burnt Umber	Maple Syrup
Deep Blush	Red Iron Oxide + Crimson	Oxblood	Poppy Red + Burnt Sienna
Deep Sage	Dark Jungle	Avocado	Olive Green
Dusty Green	Alpine	Green Mist, Arbor Green	Shamrock + White
Light Lime	White + Lime Green + Bright Yellow	White + Bright Green + Lemon Yellow	White + Kelly Green + Yellow Green
Medium Lime	Lime Green + Bright Yellow + White	Bright Green + Lemon Yellow + White	Kelly Green + Yellow Light + White
Medium Turquoise	Colonial Blue + White	Desert Turquoise + White	Teal + Cobalt Blue + White
True Orange	Pumpkin	Pumpkin	Glazed Carrots
True Poppy	Orange, Poppy Orange	Cadmium Orange	Terra Cotta + Light Red Oxide
True Red	Tompte Red	Santa Red	Napthol Crimson

Metric Conversion Chart

Inches	MM	CM	Inches	CM	Inches	CM	Inches	CM
⅛	3	0.9	6	15.2	21	53.3	36	91.4
¼	6	0.6	7	17.8	22	55.9	37	94.0
⅜	10	1.0	8	20.3	23	58.4	38	96.5
½	13	1.3	9	22.9	24	61.0	39	99.1
⅝	16	1.6	10	25.4	25	63.5	40	101.6
¾	19	1.9	11	27.9	26	66.0	41	104.1
⅞	22	2.2	12	30.5	27	68.6	42	106.7
1	25	2.5	13	33.0	28	71.1	43	109.2
1¼	32	3.2	14	35.6	29	73.7	44	111.8
1½	38	3.8	15	38.1	30	76.2	45	114.3
1¾	44	4.4	16	40.6	31	78.7	46	116.8
2	51	5.1	17	43.2	32	81.3	47	119.4
3	76	7.6	18	45.7	33	83.8	48	121.9
4	102	10.2	19	48.3	34	86.4	49	124.5
5	127	12.7	20	50.8	35	88.9	50	127.0

Index

#1 Leaf Worksheet, 88
#2 Leaf Worksheet, 88
Acorn Worksheet, 77
Angel Trumpet Leaf Worksheet, 60
Angel Trumpet Potting Table, 57–61
Angel Trumpet Potting Table Patterns, 124–125
Angel Trumpet Worksheet, 59
Autumn Leaf Worksheet, 76
Autumn Leaves Hutch, 74–77
Autumn Leaves Hutch Patterns, 132
Basic Painting Techniques, 11–15
Berries & Vines Twig Shelves, 78–81
Blossom Leaf Worksheet, 69
Blossom Worksheet, 69–70
Branch Worksheet, 77
Butterfly Worksheet, 104
Clover Leaf Worksheet, 113
Dahlia Worksheet, 87
Daisy Worksheet, 72
Fanciful Stroke Flower Worksheet, 112
Faux Tile Table, 23–29 & 36–39
Faux Tile Table Large Fruit Patterns, 116
Faux Tile Table Small Fruit Patterns, 119
Finishing, 17
Florals on Antiqued Finish Worksheet, 48
Florals on Faux Finish Worksheet, 49
Flower Leaf Worksheet, 50
Flower Worksheet, 52–53
Flowered Washstand Birdbath, 50–53
Flowered Washstand Birdbath Patterns, 122
Folk Art Tables, 45–49
Folk Art Tables Pattern, 121

Gaillardia & Bud Worksheet, 84–86
Gaillardia & Dahlia Washtubs, 82–88
Gaillardia & Dahlia Washtubs Pattern, 133
Geranium & Bud Worksheet, 42
Geranium Leaf & Pod Worksheet, 43
Geranium Planter, 40–44
Geranium Planter Pattern, 120
Grape Leaf Worksheet, 31
Grapes Worksheet, 31
Hydrangea Door, 54–56
Hydrangea Door Pattern, 123
Hydrangea Worksheet, 56
Introduction, 5
Large Apple Worksheet, 26
Large Cherry Worksheet, 28
Large Fruit Instructions, 26–29
Large Pear Worksheet, 28
Large Plum Worksheet, 27
Large Rose Worksheet, 70–71
Large Tulip Leaf Worksheet, 65–66
Large Tulip Worksheet, 64
Metric Conversion Chart, 143
Morning Glory & Bud Worksheet, 20
Morning Glory Leaf Worksheet, 22
Oversized Grapes Chair, 30–32
Oversized Grapes Chair Pattern, 117
Oversized Strawberries Chair, 33–35
Oversized Strawberries Chair Pattern, 118
Paint Conversion Chart, 141–143
Painting Tips, 16–17
Patio Storage Cabinet, 105–113
Patio Storage Cabinet Patterns, 140
Pompon Leaf Worksheet, 110
Pompon Worksheet, 108

Poppy Worksheet, 102
Poppies Bench, 100–104
Poppies Bench Pattern, 138
Poppies Bench Stamp Patterns, 139
Ray Flower Leaf Worksheet, 112
Ray Flower Worksheet, 111
Reed & Cattail Worksheet, 96
Romantic Roses Bench, 89–93
Romantic Roses Bench Pattern, 134
Romantic Roses Stencil Pattern, 135
Rose Leaf Worksheet, 93
Rose Worksheet, 91–92
Rustic Morning Glory Birdhouse, 18–22
Rustic Morning Glory Birdhouse Patterns, 114–115
Second-hand Chic Table, 67–73
Second-hand Chic Table Patterns, 127–132
Small Apple Worksheet, 37
Small Cherry Worksheet, 38
Small Fruit Instructions, 36–39
Small Pear Worksheet, 38
Small Plum Worksheet, 39
Small Rose & Bud Worksheet, 71
Small Tulip Leaf Worksheet, 52
Small Tulip Worksheet, 53
Strawberry Leaf Worksheet, 35
Strawberry Worksheet, 34
Supplies, 8–10
Surface Preparation, 15–16
Tile Instructions, 24–25
Trout Worksheet, 97–98
Tulip Pedestal, 62–66
Tulip Pedestal Pattern, 126
Vines, Leaves & Berries Worksheet, 80
Water Foliage Worksheet, 97
Wood-burned Trout Table, 94–99
Wood-burned Trout Table Patterns, 136–137